Theodorus Bailey Myers Mason

The War on the Pacific Coast of South America

Theodorus Bailey Myers Mason

The War on the Pacific Coast of South America

ISBN/EAN: 9783742864093

Manufactured in Europe, USA, Canada, Australia, Japa

Cover: Foto ©ninafisch / pixelio.de

Theodorus Bailey Myers Mason

The War on the Pacific Coast of South America

War Series, No. II.

INFORMATION FROM ABROAD.

THE WAR

ON THE

PACIFIC COAST OF SOUTH AMERICA

BETWEEN

CHILE

AND THE ALLIED REPUBLICS OF

PERU AND BOLIVIA.

1879-'81.

WASHINGTON, D. C., *July* 10, 1883.

SIR: I have the honor to submit the following account of the war on the Pacific coast of South America between Chile and the allied Republics of Peru and Bolivia.

The material for the paper has been derived from personal observation, from apparently authentic publications, from the Reports of Lieutenant-Commanders D. W. Mullan and J. J. Brice, and Lieutenants J. B. Briggs and N. T. Houston, and from the notes of Lieutenant-Commanders J. E. Craig and M. B. Buford, and Lieutenants J. F. Meigs, R. R. Ingersoll, and R. P. Rodgers.

Very respectfully,

THEO. B. M. MASON,
Lieutenant.

Hon. W. E. CHANDLER,
Secretary of the Navy.

INDEX.

	Page.
I.—The origin of the war	5
II.—Geographical and military status of the belligerents	8
III.—Naval strength of the belligerents	13
IV.—Preparations for war	21
V.—From the declaration of war, April 2, 1879, to the naval battle of Iquiqui, May 12, 1879	28
VI.—From the re-establishment of the blockade of Iquiqui to the battle of Angamos, October 8, 1879	35
VII.—From the landing at Pisagua, November 2, 1879, to the landing at Pacocha, February 24, 1880	49
VIII.—From the landing at Pacocha to the capture of Arica, June 5, 1880	53
IX.—From the fall of Arica to the fall of Lima, January 17, 1881	66

ERRATA.—WAR SERIES No. II.

Page 33, 2d line, for "70-pounders" read "riflemen."

Page 39, 17th line, for "passed through" read "entered."

THE WAR ON THE PACIFIC COAST OF SOUTH AMERICA.

I.

THE ORIGIN OF THE WAR.

The war in which the three leading republics of the Pacific coast of South America have been engaged commenced on the 2d of April, 1879, and has extended to the present period.

Like most of the countries of Central and South America, Chile, Peru, and Bolivia were settled by the Spaniards, who deserve credit for their energy as pioneers of civilization.

Of the three countries, that known as Peru seems by far the most attractive. Its climate was the mildest; its land, at a short distance from the coast, the most fertile; its mineral wealth the most evident and obtainable. It was thickly populated by a mild and industrious race of Indians, if we can believe the historians and the proof furnished on every side by ruins, aqueducts, roads, and terraced mountain sides.

Chile, on the contrary, was apparently less inviting, and was inhabited by a hardy, warlike race.

Bolivia, lying inland, detached by a range of high mountains and inhabited by warlike tribes, presented few attractions to the Spaniards, and to this day her race has preserved many of its original characteristics.

During the rebellion against the mother country, in the early part of this century, Chile was the first of the Pacific colonies to gain her independence. This accomplished, her people, aided by that indomitable Scotchman, Lord Cochrane, and a small but well-trained band of his countrymen and of our own, went to the assistance of their Peruvian neighbors. The freedom of Peru was due mainly to this timely aid.

The Spaniards who remained in Peru after the first conquest were principally military men, who made themselves the proprietors of all of its wealth.

As the first settlers were accompanied by few women, they were forced to marry Indian women, thus founding a mixed race. The introduction of negroes to supply the places of the Indians who had either died or withdrawn to the interior, and also that of the Chinese coolies, to replace the negroes who had become affected by the change of condition, still further affected the character of the people.

During the colonial days many Spaniards, with their families, came to the country, most of them in the employ of the Government, a few, however, as *bona-fide* colonists, and their descendants to-day constitute an element of the Peruvian nation; they are generally planters. It is to be regretted that a large number of them has left the country, probably never to return.

The colonial government was administered either by Spaniards *pur sang* or by the mesclados.

The Indians have withdrawn to the interior, where they remain unless brought to the coast as soldiers, sailors, or servants. Commerce, trade, and industry tempted many foreigners to the country. The trade has fallen mostly into the hands of Italians, Germans, French, and Jews, commerce into those of the English, speculative enterprises of all kinds to our countrymen, and the hard work to negroes, Chinese, and Chilians. There are no manufactures, goods of all kinds being imported.

Chile is a narrow strip of country lying between the mountains and the sea; it had been colonized by a hardier set of Spaniards, equally desirous with their brothers in Peru to profit by their adventurousness. Like their neighbors they brought the aborigines under subjection, but made them their co-workers, and sought to educate them. This retention and elevation of the lower classes prevented the necessity of introducing large numbers of foreign laborers and made the Chilian race purer and more homogeneous. The country did not attract many speculators. The foreigners who settled in it came to work, and finding an unprejudiced, liberal-minded, intelligent people, intermarried with them, so that they became more than personally interested in the welfare of the country, and by degrees gave its people so much of the caste of a northern nation that the Chilians of to-day are known as the Yankees of South America. Not finding sufficient occupation or remuneration within their own boundaries, many Chilians, both capitalists and laborers, began to look for employment for their funds and energies elsewhere. The English, Chilian, and American companies, engaged in developing the mineral wealth of Peru and in constructing her railroads, besides shareholders and directors, found most of their laborers in Chile. The steamship companies and owners of sailing vessels employed in the coast trade drew their crews from the same source. Many even enlisted in the Peruvian navy. The Chilian Nitrate Company succeeded and competed with the Peruvian Government in the fertilizer trade.

Bolivia lies, with the exception of a short strip of sea-coast, in the interior of the continent, and is inhabited by almost full-breed Indians, warlike in their nature.

The cause of the war grew out of this condition of affairs, and was as follows:

The province of Atacama, or more properly the desert of Atacama, had remained for many years without a definite owner, at one time claimed by Bolivia, at another by Chile, but never considered of sufficient importance to warrant the establishment of a boundary line until the discovery of the guano, nitrates and other mineral wealth which it contained. In 1866, the republics being allied in war against their common enemy Spain, a treaty between Bolivia and Chile established the boundary at the 24th parallel of south latitude, and further stipulated that Chilian citizens already land owners between the parallels of 23° and 24° south should be allowed to mine and export the valuable products without tax or hinderance from the Government of Bolivia. To facilitate the execution of this agreement Chile was allowed to have a representative in the custom-house at Antofagasta. The nitrate business was chiefly in the hands of a company, the principal parties in which were the English house of Gibbs, a Chilian named Edwards, and the Chilian Government; on the 23d of February, 1878, Bolivia levied a tax of ten centavos per quintal on all nitrates. When remonstrated with for this alleged breach of treaty stipulations, the Bolivian Government not only refused to remit the tax but declared it retroactive, and further decreed that if the taxes were not paid before the 14th of February, 1879, the nitrates in the hands of the exporters should be seized and sold at auction. Chile remonstrated against these proceedings, and sent her fleet, under Rear-Admiral Rebolledo Williams, to protect the property of her citizens at Antofagasta. This fleet arrived on the day fixed for the seizure.

On the 24th of January the Chilian Government formally ordered the occupation of Antofagasta, which was equivalent to a declaration of war with Bolivia. On the day on which this order was issued 500 Chilian regulars were landed at Antofagasta, which became the headquarters for further operations. Colonel Sotomayor was afterwards sent to Caracoles to protect the mining interests with his troops. On March 23d a fight occurred at Calama between this column and a body of Bolivians under Dr. Ladislao Cabrera, in which the latter were defeated and forced to retire with a loss of 20 killed or wounded and 30 prisoners, including one colonel and two other officers. The Chilian loss in killed and wounded was 12 men. Peru sent envoys to La Paz, the capital of Bolivia, and Santiago, the capital of Chile. Chile demanded of Peru the reasons for her preparations for war and that they should cease. Not being satisfied with the answer, Chile, on the 2d of April, formally declared war, and at the same time asserted that she knew of a secret treaty of February 6, 1873, between Peru and Bolivia.

II.

GEOGRAPHICAL AND MILITARY STATUS OF THE BELLIGERENTS.

The continent of South America is divided into two water-sheds by the Andes Mountains, which extend from the Isthmus of Panama south to the Straits of Magellan. The western water-shed is extremely narrow, not exceeding 300 miles in its widest part. Owing to the scarcity of rain, especially between the latitudes of Coquimbo and the Guayaquil River, it is arid in the extreme. At rare intervals small streams, almost dry in the southern summer months, flow from the mountains to the sea. These streams have formed valleys that in some cases are very fertile, though separated from each other by dreary and almost impassable wastes of desert. In these valleys is congregated most of the population, and through many of them enterprising foreigners have constructed railways, establishing in some cases communication with the rich eastern water-shed. The coast line is very regular, trending for long distances in the same direction without dangerous headlands or outlying rocks. The reefs are close inshore, and do not present any obstacle to navigation. High bluffs separate the deserts from the ocean, and where the valleys extend to the sea broad plains are found. With the exception of Valdivia, Valparaiso, Coquimbo, Mejillones de Bolivia, Callao, Chimbote, and Paita, there are no harbors in the countries of which we wish to treat. The other ports are open roadsteads and mere landing places for small boats. Some of the latter are reached through narrow passages in the reefs, some by running through the surf, and others can only be effected by means of baskets or cages let down from high iron piers or even from the cliffs themselves. The winds on the coast are very regular, blowing with almost uniform force from south to north. With the exception of occasional northers in the southern winter season, seldom reaching even then north of Valparaiso, gales are unknown. During some seasons heavy fogs rise at night and continue until about 11 a. m. This is especially the case about Callao. The harbors are large, and excepting that of Valparaiso, which is open to the northers, are safe. They are basins and are easy of approach, there being no bars. In view of these facts it will be readily understood that the most direct communication between the valleys must be by sea, and that with the interior, through the valleys. Thus limited, the military question of attack and defense became very simple, and may be stated in five words, *the command of the sea*. President Adams's remark to Commodore Truxtun, that "Neptunes' trident is the scepter of the world," was exemplified, as far as this portion of its surface is concerned.

Chile, the southernmost of the three belligerents, lies entirely to the westward of the Andes, and in no place exceeds 200 miles in width. It extends from 24° south latitude nominally to the Straits of Magellan. The country north of the port of Coquimbo, 29° 30' south, the present southern limit of the rainless belt, is arid in the extreme. South of Coquimbo it improves until it assumes quite a promising aspect at Talcahuana and Valdivia. The population of Chile in 1879 numbered about 2,100,000. The principal sea-ports, none of which are naturally adapted for defense, are Valdivia; Talcahuana, the sea-port of Concepcion, connected with it and Santiago by rail; Valparaiso, a large city, but also the sea-port of Santiago, the capital, with which it is connected by rail; Coquimbo, connected by rail with La Serena; Huasco, and Caldera.

The Andes, fortunately for Chile, form an excellent western boundary line for the Argentine Republic. Chile and the Argentine Republic, until lately, have been continually at variance on the boundary question, and it is possible that the two allies who were to be arrayed against Chile expected valuable aid from the Argentines.

Chile, through the industry and enterprise of her inhabitants, is almost self-supporting. Beef is the only absolute necessary of life that has to be imported. Most of this is driven across the mountains on the hoof from pampas.

Bolivia, with the exception of a small extent of sea-coast from the 21st to the 24th degree of south latitude, lies to the eastward of the Andes, which range, with the almost impassable deserts to the westward, virtually isolates the more thickly populated districts, communication between them being maintained through Peru to the sea-coast and thence to Antofagasta. The interior of Bolivia is well endowed by nature, but the sea-coast is wholly arid, as there is not even a valley to redeem it. If it were not for the lately discovered mineral wealth of this region it would be an absolute wilderness. As it is, the Chilians in search of riches have surmounted some of its difficulties, and have built a railway from Antofagasta towards the Caracoles mining district. There is no harbor at Antofagasta, and on account of dangerous reefs and a narrow channel communication with the shore is effected by boats. As in many other mining ports on the coast, fresh water is distilled from sea-water. Mejillones de Bolivia, as it is called, to distinguish it from another Mejillones, is a small settlement of workmen employed in the guano deposits that lie near it. The inhabitants of this part of Bolivia, except a few soldiers and office-holders, are Chilians. Geographically this province should belong to Chile, whose natural boundary is the river Loa; while the natural outlet of Bolivia to the sea is through the Peruvian departments of Moquegua and Arequipa. Bolivia is self-supplying as to the necessaries of life. It has been impossible to obtain reliable statistics of the population of this country, but it may be stated as approximately between two and three millions.

Peru, a country nearly three times as large as France, extends from the river Loa to the mouth of the Guayaquil, and from the ocean to near the middle of the continent, where it borders upon Brazil. The narrow strip of territory lying between the Andes and the ocean resembles the northern part of Chile and the coast province of Bolivia. East of the mountains the country is as beautiful and as fertile as any on the globe. The magnificent steppes of the Andes and the plains and valleys at the headwaters of the Amazon, if properly colonized and governed, would alone make Peru one of the richest countries in the world. It was to open up this territory that the Oroya Railway was planned and partially constructed by our countryman, Henry Meiggs, ably assisted by his brother John and a large staff of American engineers. This roadway, which has an average grade of 4 feet in 100, follows the valley of the Rimac from Callao, through Lima and a number of small towns, winding along and up the faces of precipices by cuts, V-shaped curves, and all manner of loops; over bridges spanning chasms in some cases a thousand feet deep, some built at once on a grade and a curve; through tunnels of great length; making miles of detour to gain one of advance, and finally piercing, with a tunnel 4,000 feet long, the very backbone of the Andes, 15,645 feet above the level of the sea. Over 86 of the 136 miles necessary to reach the town of Oroya are already open to traffic. The roadway is prepared as far as the summit, and, had peace reigned, in a few years more the coffers of Peru would be filling from this new and almost inexhaustible region. American enterprise is now trying to open a way to this district by steamer up the Amazon and then by rail through the valleys of its tributaries. The principal sea-ports of Peru are Iquiqui and Pisagua, both situated on the edge of the desert of Tarapaca, and connected by rail with the nitrate deposits of that province. Neither of these places has a harbor, and each has to be supplied with water by artificial means. Arica, another port without a harbor, is the sea terminus of an important railway running to Tacna, from which a highroad leads to La Paz, the capital of Bolivia. Ilo and Mollendo are mere landing places, the first being the outlet of the rich valley of Moquegua, with the city of which name it is connected by rail, the second that of Arequipa and of Puno on Lake Titicaca. This road is another of Meiggs's masterpieces in engineering, and is the main line of communication between Bolivia and the sea. Pisco, with a moderately good harbor, is connected by rail with the inland city of Ica. Callao, with its dependent ports of Chorillos and Ancon, is the sea-port of Lima. Chancay is a landing-place, connected through Ancon with Lima by the only *coast* railroad in Peru. There is also railway communication between the excellent harbor of Chimbote and the village of Huaraz; between Salaberry, the landing-place of Trujillo, and Trujillo itself; and between the fine harbor of Paita—the old rendezvous of the whaling fleet—and the city of Piura.

An English company had constructed a submarine telegraph line from Callao to Valparaiso, with branches to the important intermediate points. The Callao terminus was connected with Paita by a shore line, which was rarely in working order. That at Valparaiso was connected by a trans-Andean line with Buenos Ayres, whence there was connection with the United States. This line introduced a new feature in this war, hitherto unprovided for in the law of nations. At the Congress of the Institute of International Law, held at Brussels in September, 1879, the following resolution was adopted:

1. It would be well if the several powers would declare the destruction of submarine cables on the high seas an infraction of the law of nations, and determine the penalty of the offense. On this last point such uniformity should be attained as would conform with the different criminal codes.
2. The right to seize guilty or suspected individuals should be given to all men-of-war, with the restrictions determined by treaty; but the right of jurisdiction should be vested in the Government of the accused.
3. A submarine cable between two neutral territories should be inviolable.
4. It is to be desired that when telegraphic communication should cease on account of a state of war, sequestration should replace destruction. At any rate, destruction should be practiced in a very limited degree, and the belligerent who should resort to it should restore the cable communication as quickly as possible after the termination of the war.

Chile had in her presidential chair Don Annibal Pinto.
Bolivia was ruled by General Hilarion Daza.
The President of Peru was Mariano I. Prado.
The Chilian regular army had never exceeded 3,500 men of all arms. In 1879 it numbered—

Infantry	1,500
Artillery	410
Cavalry	530
Total	2,440

Besides the regulars, each city had a uniformed body of militia; that of Valparaiso forming a brigade of infantry, which would have compared very favorably with like troops in our own country.

The regulars were recruited from the Indian element principally, and were as fine a body of men in general appearance and discipline as could be found in any army in the world, suggesting very forcibly the possibility of utilizing our own Indians in the same way. The Chilian officers, not enjoying the advantages of a technical education, and possessing but limited knowledge of military operations beyond barrack-yard evolutions, were relatively not as efficient as the men. The tactics and manual were modeled on those of the Spanish for muzzle-loading weapons, and were not adapted to the use of modern fire-arms. The men were well clothed, the uniforms resembling in color and fashion those of the French army; in fact, many of them were manufactured by Godillot, in Paris; the equipments were old-fashioned, and were found so badly adapted to the requirements of modern warfare that after a short experience they were replaced by others more suited to the period, and which will be described in another place.

The infantry (regular) had just been armed with the Comblain rifle, manufactured in Belgium. This arm resembles the Sharp rifle, with its movable block, the only difference being the union of the block and its appendages with the breech-block. The metal used in the manufacture of the breech-block, bands, &c., was phosphoric bronze, which, when cast into shape, required but little finishing. The artillery was armed with obsolete guns, although a few Krupp rifles were in store. The cavalry was armed with French sabers and Comblain carbines.

According to apparently reliable sources, the Bolivian regular army numbered 2,300 men and 1,000 officers.

The uniforms of the men were made of a material resembling gunny cloth, coarsely dyed in imitation of the French uniform. The arms were of the most obsolete type, several battalions being provided with flint-lock muskets.

The standing army of Peru, including the gendarmerie and Lima police, has been variously estimated at from 9,000 to 13,000 men of all arms. As in most Spanish countries, each corps was known by a name instead of a number. The following is a summary of the regular troops, as given in Señor Paz-Soldan's very interesting work:

INFANTRY.

Pichincha Battalion.
Ayacucho Battalion.
Callao Battalion.
Punyan Battalion.
Izuchaco Battalion.
Paucarpata Battalion.

6th of March Battalion.
7th of March Battalion.
Cuzco Battalion.
Puno Battalion.
Huancavy Battalion.

CAVALRY.

Junin Huzzars.
Tacna Mounted Rifles.

Union Lancers.
4th Provisional.

ARTILLERY.

2 light batteries mountain guns, one battalion.

1 battery siege guns.

Most of these troops were collected in and about Lima. They were recruited largely from the Cholo or Indian element, but there was also a large number of negroes and mesclados, who were easily incited to revolution, and it was through them that the succeeding aspirants for power accomplished their designs.

Until a short time previous to the declaration of war the troops were uniformed in the French style; it was then decided to adopt the German dress, and some corps had already received their new clothing. The regulars were armed with the French Chassepot rifle. Besides the regular army, a very respectable corps of militia was maintained in the larger cities. The tactics and manual were of the Spanish system. There were no engineer troops.

III.

THE NAVAL STRENGTH OF THE BELLIGERENTS.

The Chilian navy had been fostered by the Government, which was fully alive to the vital importance of this branch of the national defense, surrounded as Chile was by nations more or less hostile, but who, owing to her natural defenses of mountains and deserts, would be forced to attack her by sea. Willing to profit by the costly experiments carried on in other countries, and having no home interests to protect, she sent her officers abroad—the older ones to examine the latest ships and guns, the younger ones to enter the foreign services and gain experience in their duties. The result has been that she has added to her fleet two fine English-built iron-clads of the very best sea-going type, an excellent corvette, and a corps of young officers well suited to handle them.

The Chilian navy is administered by a minister of the marine, who is also minister of war. General B. Arrutia held the office at the outbreak of the war.

The *personnel* of the regular navy was as follows:

Vice-admiral	1	
Rear-admirals (*contra almirante*)	3	
Captains (*capitan de navio*)	3	
Commanders (*capitan de fragata*)	12	
Lieutenant-commanders (*capitan de corbeta*)	14	
Lieutenants (*teniente de primera classe*)	18	
Masters (*teniente de segunda classe*)	25	
Midshipmen (*guardia marina*)	39	
Cadet-midshipmen (*aspirante*)	30	
		145
Senior surgeon (*medico major*)	1	
Surgeons (*primero medico*)	9	
		10
Inspector of machinery	1	
Engineers of the 1st class	7	
Engineers of the 2d class	10	
Engineers of the 3d class	20	
		38
Pay inspector	1	
Paymaster of the 1st class	5	
Paymaster of the 2d class	3	
		9
Pilots		6
		203
Enlisted men (*tripulantes*)		1,500
Total		1,708

There was, besides, a corps of marines, who, when ashore, formed part of the regular army.

The *matériel* of the navy consisted of the armored, box casemated, sea-going rams Almirante Cochrane and Blanco Encalada (formerly Valparaiso), both designed by Sir E. J. Reed, M. P., and considered by him among his best conceptions; built by Earle's Shipbuilding Company, at Hull, England, in 1874; engines constructed by John Penn & Sons; cost of each, about $1,000,000 in gold. Their length between perpendiculars was 210 feet; beam, 45 feet 9 inches; draught, forward, 18 feet 8 inches—aft, 19 feet 8 inches; height of battery above water-line, 5 feet 6 inches; displacement, 3,560 tons; engines, two pair, compound, horizontal trunk; horse-power, 2,960; screw-propellers, 2; speed, measured mile, 12.8 knots.

The armament consists of six 9-inch 12-ton muzzle-loading Armstrong rifles, mounted on Scott muzzle-pivoting carriages, in a central-box battery, with double re-entering forward and after ports, this arrangement permitting the forward gun on each side a train from right ahead to abeam, the central gun from 70° forward of the beam to 35° abaft the beam, and the after one from abeam to right astern. Each ship carried, besides, one 20-pounder, one 9-pounder, and one 7-pounder. The Blanco Encalada carries two 1-inch ½-pounder Nordenfelt machine guns, one on each end of the bridge, and the Almirante Cochrane one mounted on the knight-heads forward. After the battle of Angamos several Hotchkiss revolving guns were added to the armaments for use against torpedoes. In addition to these light guns, 12 picked riflemen in action are stationed in the fore and main tops, protected from observation by screens. The battery is 7½ feet high, the armor is in two strakes, the lower of which is 8 inches and the upper 6 inches thick on the sides and forward part, while on the after part both have a uniform thickness of 4½ inches. The armor is backed by about 14 inches of teak, inside of which is a thin iron skin. The armored transverse bulkheads forming the forward and after ends of the casemate extend below the water-line. The iron double-bottomed hull is divided by seven water-tight transverse bulkheads, and is protected around the water-line by an armor-belt 9 feet wide in three strakes. The middle strake is 9 inches thick amidships, while the other two are 6 inches, all of them tapering to a uniform thickness of 4½ inches at bow and stern. The teak backing behind the armor-belt has an average thickness of 10 inches, and the whole of the armor and backing is fastened to a double thickness of skin plating, supported by massive angle-iron frames on the inside, and longitudinal angle-iron guides on the outside. The upper deck, which is flush with the upper edge of the armor-belt, is protected by 3 inches of armor near the casemate and 2 inches at the bow and stern. The casemate overhangs the side about 3 feet.

It is reported that these vessels when in good condition make 10 knots per hour on a coal consumption of from 30 to 35 tons per day. Their coal-bunker capacity is 254 tons. They are bark-rigged, and have a complement of 300 men. They can fire their guns by electricity, and their steam launches, of ordinary type, are fitted to carry spar torpedoes. Beside its regular armament each carries a rocket tube and rockets. Neither is fitted for torpedoes.

The stem is a solid casting, ram-shaped, and strengthened by backing and bracing. The ram extends 7 feet 6 inches beyond the bow, and the point is 6 feet 9 inches below the water-line. Condition of the hulls, good; Blanco's bottom very foul; Cochrane's better, as she had been taken to England to be docked and cleaned. The Blanco's bottom is sheathed with wood and zinc.

The corvettes O'Higgins and Chacabuco, wooden hulls, built in England in 1867. Length between perpendiculars, 217 feet; beam, 35 feet; mean draught, 15 feet 9 inches; displacement, 1,670 tons; engines, simple, old type; screw, single and lifting; speed, 8 to 10 knots; rig, ship; armament, three 7-ton muzzle-loading Armstrong rifles, on pivot carriages; two 70-pounder muzzle-loading Armstrong rifles, in broadside; four 40-pounder muzzle-loading Armstrong rifles, broadside; number of crew, 160 men; condition, hulls fair; boilers very old and poor.

The corvette Abtao, built in England, 1864. Hull, wood; displacement, 1,050 tons; engines, simple, old style; horse-power, 300; screw, single; speed 5 to 6 knots; armament, three 150-pounder muzzle-loading Armstrong rifles, on pivot carriages; three 30-pounder muzzle-loading Armstrong rifles, two in broadside, one on pivot carriages; rig, bark; condition: hull poor; engines so defective that she had been sold to private parties, who had removed them in order to convert her into a sailing vessel. Repurchased engines and boilers replaced.

The sloop of war Esmeralda, built in England in 1854. Hull, wood; length between perpendiculars, 200 feet; beam, 35 feet; draught, 14 feet; tonnage, old measurement, 850 tons; engines, simple, old type; nominal horse-power, 200; screw, single and lifting; speed, 3 knots; rig, ship; armament: original, eight 40-pounder muzzle-loading Armstrong rifles, in broadside, increased to fourteen 40-pounder muzzle-loading Armstrong rifles, broadside; crew, 160 men; condition of hull, old and rotten; boilers, very old and almost unserviceable.

The second-class corvette Magellanes, built in England, 1874. Hull, composite; length between perpendiculars, 190 feet; beam, 27 feet; mean draught, 13 feet; displacement, 772 tons; engines, compound; twin screws; horse-power, 1,230; speed, 11 knots per hour, on 24 tons coal per day; rig, barkentine; armament, one 7-ton muzzle-loading Armstrong rifle, on pivot carriage; one 64-pounder muzzle-loading Armstrong rifle, on pivot carriage; one 20-pounder muzzle-loading Armstrong rifle, on pivot carriage; condition, excellent; cruising under Commander Latórre in the Straits of Magellan.

The gunboat Covadonga, captured from the Spaniards in 1866 by the Esmeralda. Tonnage, old measurement, 412; engines, old style, 140 horse-power; single screw; maximum speed, 5 knots; rig, three-masted topsail schooner; condition: hull poor; engines and boilers poor; armament, two 70-pounder muzzle-loading Armstrong rifles, on pivot carriages.

The small side-wheel tender Tolten, carrying a few light guns.

Besides these men-of-war, Chile had an excellent line of English-built coast steamers and a number of steamers engaged in transporting ores, &c., belonging to the Cousiño estate.

There is no regular navy-yard, although one has been projected and will probably be completed, as the experiences of the war have shown its necessity. There are several large machine shops at Valparaiso, one of which, belonging to the Pacific Steam Navigation Company, is particularly well adapted for repairs to steam machinery. In the harbor of Valparaiso are two large floating docks, capable of raising the smaller vessels, but not of sufficient strength for the heavy iron-clads. There is an arsenal for naval stores at Valparaiso, where there are also a limited number of workshops for slight repairs.

Chile has a naval school where the young officers of the line are educated. She has also a naval observatory and a hydrographic office, whose publications are excellent. The smaller vessels of the fleet were employed in surveying the Chilian coast, Smythe's Channel, and the Straits of Magellan.

The Cochrane was sent to England a year before the war for some slight alterations and to have her bottom cleaned.

The uniform of the Chilian navy is modeled after our own, which it resembled in almost every particular before we adopted broad stripes.

The book of regulations is almost identical with ours of 1876. A private modification of the present international code of signals is used for communicating between vessels.

The supply of coals is drawn almost entirely from Wales and Australia, Chilian coal not being adapted for steaming purposes, as it fuses and clogs the grates.

The crews of the Chilian ships are drawn mostly from the Indian element; there is, however, a considerable number of foreigners, as is usual in all services recruited by volunteers. The discipline and instruction of the men were very fair, and the first naval action of the war proved that target practice had not been neglected.

Bolivia has no naval force.

The Peruvian navy was controlled by a minister of the marine, who was also minister of war. Immediately after the last war with Spain, the Government felt the necessity of a modern addition to its naval force, and sent a commission to Europe to examine foreign navies, and contract for two iron-clads and two fast corvettes. Another commission was sent to the United States, which had just then emerged from the great rebellion. The result was the purchase of the Huascar and Independencia in England, the Manco Capac and Atahualpa in the United States, and the Union and America in France. The last two had been built for our southern states in rebellion. The America, similar in all respects to the Union, was lost in the great tidal wave at Arica. Since this infusion of new material nothing has been added to the Peruvian navy, except the little transport Talisman, which belonged to the Pierolista party, and came from England loaded with arms for the revolution of May, 1877. It may be interesting here for many reasons to retrospect a little and give a description of one of the events of this revolution. Chief Engineer King, in his useful work, The War Ships and Navies of the World, gives a graphic account of this action, which is herein repeated.

In speaking of the engagement that occurred in the Pacific, off the bay of Ilo, May 29, 1877, between the British unarmored vessel Shah assisted by the corvette Amethyst, and the Peruvian iron-clad Huascar, he says:

This action, if worthy to be called by that name, was brought about by very strange procedures on the part of the officers of the Huascar. The gist of the reports is as follows: During a revolution, common to South American Governments, the adherents of an insurgent leader, Nicolas de Pierola, persuaded the officers of the Huascar to rebel against the Peruvian Government, and with their consent a number of these men seized the vessel in the harbor of Callao, under the cover of darkness, and put to sea, sailing to the southward. At Cobija, in Bolivia, Pierola embarked on the Huascar, which then steamed to the north with a view to effect a landing. Very shortly after this the Shah, with Rear-Admiral de Horsey on board, arrived at Callao, and being informed of the above facts, also that depredations had been committed by the Huascar on British property and against British subjects, Admiral de Horsey made complaint to the Peruvian Government, and receiving in response a decree declaring the Huascar a pirate, offering a reward for her capture, and repudiating all responsibility on the part of Peru for acts committed by her, he determined to proceed against the Huascar with his flag ship the Shah, and the Amethyst. Having put to sea for this purpose, he sighted the Huascar off the town of Ilo on the afternoon of May 29, and summoned her to surrender. This summons the commanding officer refused to entertain. The Shah then fired, first a blank cartridge, and then a shotted charge, but the Huascar still refusing to surrender, a steady and well-sustained fire from both the Shah and Amethyst was directed against her. The fight was partly in chase and partly circular, the distance between the combatants being for the greater part of the time from 1,500 to 2,500 yards. The time employed in the engagement was about three hours, the fight being terminated by darkness coming on and the Huascar running close inshore where the Shah could not follow, consequent upon her greater draught. Of the projectiles thrown from the English ships it is reported that some seventy or eighty struck the iron-clad, principally about the upper decks, bridge, masts, and boats; one projectile from the heavy gun pierced the side on the port quarter 2 feet above the water, where the armor was $2\frac{1}{4}$ or 3 inches thick, and brought up against the opposite side, killing one man and wounding another; two other projectiles dented in the side armor to the extent of 3 inches. The turret was struck once by a projectile from the heavy guns of the Shah; it was a direct blow, but penetrated 3 inches only. The hull showed that several 64-pounder shot had struck it, only leaving marks. When at close quarters, which the Huascar sought for the purpose of ramming, the Gatling gun in the Shah's foretop drove the men from the quarter-deck guns of the former. On one of these occasions a Whitehead torpedo was launched at the iron-clad, but as she altered her course about the same instant the torpedo failed to strike its mark.

Although it has been asserted that the Huascar's turret was struck normally by a 247-pound shot, it would hardly seem possible that such could have been the weight of the projectile, because others of about the same weight have since pierced the same turret when striking at a slight angle. Owing to the entire absence of even ordinarily instructed gunners on board the Huascar, the English ships were not struck by the turret guns, and only a 40-pounder shot passed through their rigging. Had this not been the case the result might have been appalling. As it is, this should prove a very useful lesson to us who are not as well prepared, either in ships, guns, or knowledge of handling such ships and guns, as the English were.

There being no sea-going natives amongst the Peruvians, they were forced to rely almost entirely on foreigners recruited in Callao to man their ships. These were the off-scouring of foreign merchant and naval services, the best among them being Chilians. This material filled the ratings of seamen and ordinary seamen, and supplied the petty officers. The landsmen were native Cholos. The best officers in the world could not have made anything out of such material. The active navy was commanded by Rear-Admiral de la Haza, who had his headquarters established in the Callao arsenal.

The material of the fleet was as follows:

The iron-clad ram frigate Independencia, built by Samuda, at Poplar on Thames, England, in 1864. Hull iron, divided into three water-tight compartments; length, 215 feet; beam, 44 feet 9 inches; draught forward, 21 feet 6 inches—aft, 22 feet 6 inches; height of battery above water-line, 10 feet; displacement, 2,004 tons; machinery by John Penn & Sons, old type; indicated horse-power, 1,500; maximum speed on trial, April 27, 1879, 12 knots; coal capacity, 400 tons; armament, two 150-pounder muzzle-loading Armstrong rifles on spar-deck pivots; twelve 70-pounder muzzle-loading Armstrong rifles in broadside, on a clear gun-deck. To this, at the outbreak of the war, were added one 250-pounder muzzle-loading Vavasseur rifle on pivot in bows; one 150-pounder muzzle-loading Parrott rifle on pivot in stern. Armor, $4\frac{1}{2}$ inches thick at water-line, and about central part of battery, backed by 10 inches of teak. Bow strengthened and shaped for ramming. Condition: hull good; boilers new. Rig, ship.

The iron-clad single-turret ram Huascar, built by Laird Brothers, at the Birkenhead Iron Works, England, in 1865. Hull, iron, divided into five water-tight compartments by four transverse $\frac{5}{8}$-inch iron bulkheads, with water-tight doors. These bulkheads are situated at each end of the turret chamber, fire-room, and engine-room, making separate compartments of them, and also of the forward and after part of the ship. There is also near the bow a transverse water-tight collision bulkhead to protect the vessel in case of injury from ramming. On each side of the fire-room there is a longitudinal $\frac{5}{8}$-inch iron bulkhead extending to the transverse bulkheads forward and aft, leaving a space 3 feet wide between it and the ship's side. The bottom is double. Length, 196 feet; beam, 35 feet 6 inches; depth of hold, 21 feet; free-board,

4 feet 6 inches; draught forward, 15 feet—aft, 16 feet; displacement, 1,130 tons; machinery by Laird Brothers, simple, jet condenser; screw, single, four-bladed, non-raising; indicated horse-power, 1,200; coal capacity, 300 tons; turning capacity, through 180°, 2 minutes 0.3 seconds; maximum speed, 11 knots. Armament: two 10-inch 12½-ton 300-pounder muzzle-loading Armstrong rifles, mounted in a revolving turret, placed forward. This turret is on Captain Coles's plan, being supported on rollers, and revolved by hand-gearing. The exterior diameter is 22 feet. Owing to a top-gallant forecastle forward, and the conning tower and stationary bulwarks aft, the turret guns command only 138° of the horizon; that is, from 10° on either side of the bow-line to 32° on either side of the stern-line. Two 40-pounder muzzle-loading Armstrong rifles, one on the starboard quarter-deck and one in the stern; one 12-pounder muzzle-loading Armstrong on the port-quarter deck. These light guns are all mounted on wooden Marsilly carriages. Armor: the side armor, extending 3 feet 6 inches below the load-water line, has a thickness of 4½ inches abreast the turret chamber, fire, and engine rooms, diminishing to 2½ inches at the bow and stern. This is backed by 10 inches of teak and an inner iron skin ½-inch thick. The bow is reinforced and shaped for ramming. The decks are protected by 2-inch plates. The spar-deck terminates forward in a small top-gallant forecastle, about 6 feet high, on which the anchors are secured, and in an open poop aft. The bulwarks from the forecastle to the main rigging are of iron, hinged, and are let down when clearing for action. Aft, the bulwarks are of wood and stationary, surmounted by hammock nettings. Abaft the turret was a conning tower, hexagonal in shape, 7 feet 6 inches high, and 8 feet wide by 5 feet 2 inches long. It was plated with 3-inch armor in vertical slabs, backed by balks of teak 8 inches thick, placed on end, and held in position by extending down through the deck, and by an inner frame of angle irons, to which the armor was bolted through and through. The top was unarmored, and surmounted by a bridge or walk. The upper part of each plate was pierced with long horizontal slits for sighting. Around the smoke-stack, which was unarmored, was a fire-room hatch, with a high wooden combing. The base of the smoke-stack was unprovided with a bomb-proof grating. The armor of the turret is 5½ inches thick, backed by 13 inches of teak set on end, and a ½-inch iron inner skin, except around the oval port-holes, where the thickness of the armor is increased by 2-inch plates let into the backing, which is reduced a like amount. The turret is covered with a slightly convex roof of 2-inch plates, in which there are two holes, outside and above the rear of each gun, covered with light bullet-proof hoods. These are used for laying the turret. The rudder is of the ordinary type, and is worked by a common steering-wheel under the poop, except in action, when the steering is done from a wheel placed under the conning tower on the berth-deck. Rig: brig, with movable bowsprit. The foremast was a tripod of iron tubes,

one placed nearly vertical amidships, well forward of the turret, the other two inclining aft and towards the sides. These after-legs obstructed the range of turret-fire. The mainmast was an ordinary iron mast, its rigging (wire) setting up to the rail without channels. Four boats were carried on davits, two on each side of the quarter-deck. One of these was a steam-launch.

Two single-turreted harbor and river monitors, Ericsson type, the Atahualpa and Manco Capac (formerly the United States ships Catawba and Oneota), built under the supervision of Chief Engineer J. W. King, at Cincinnati, Ohio, in 1866; bought by Peruvian Government, and were 14 months getting from New Orleans to Callao, a long delay being necessary in Rio Janeiro, caused by the refusal of the crew and officers to proceed further in the vessels. Large offers were made by the Peruvian Government for any one who would contract to take them on to Callao. Hull, iron, single bottomed; length, 235 feet; beam, 46 feet; depth of hold, 12 feet 6 inches; draught of water, mean, 13 feet 6 inches; displacement, 2,100 tons; engines, vibrating lever, single screw; maximum speed, 6 knots; indicated horse-power, 320. Armament: two cast-iron smooth-bore muzzle-loading Dahlgren 15-inch guns, mounted on Ericsson carriages in a revolving turret. Armor: laminated wrought-iron, 5 inches thick on sides, extending 5 feet below the deck; 10 inches on turret; external diameter of turret, 22 feet 8 inches; sweep of guns, all round except 40° right aft. The turret is mounted on central spindle, revolving by means of gearing driven by steam-power. The pilot-house, with fighting wheel, is over the turret. Flush deck, clear of obstructions except the smoke-stack and ventilating shaft in rear of the turret.

The wooden corvette Union, built at Nantes, France, in 1864; hull, wood; length, 243 feet; beam, 35 feet 6 inches; mean draught, 18 feet; displacement, 1,150 tons; engines, simple, 400 nominal horse-power; maximum speed, 12 knots; screw, single; armament, two 100-pounder muzzle-loading Parrott rifles, in broadside, on Marsilly carriages; two 70-pounder muzzle-loading rifles, French guns, on pivot carriages, one forward and one aft; twelve 40-pounder muzzle-loading rifles, French guns, in broadside. The Parrotts were added to her armament to the detriment of her steaming qualities, and were afterwards removed. Uncovered spar-deck, top-gallant forecastle, and poop cabin; rig, ship.

The small wooden corvette Pilcomayo; hull, wood; English-built, launched in 1864; tonnage, 600; engines, simple, 180 nominal horse-power; speed, between 10 and 11 knots; armament, two 70-pounder muzzle-loading Armstrong rifles, on pivot carriages; four 40-pounder muzzle-loading Armstrong rifles, in broadside; flush spar-deck; rig, barkentine.

The transports Chalaco and Limeña, of 1,000 and 1,163 tons displacement; armed with two 40-pounder muzzle-loadings Armstrongs; capable of steaming 11 and 12 knots. These vessels had been purchased from the Pacific Steam Navigation Company, and were used in carrying troops and officials along the coast. The upper works and cabins remained standing as in the merchant service.

The small transport Talisman, of 310 tons, and several small tugs, completed the list of available vessels.

Both Chile and Peru had quite a large number of hulks, the remains of obsolete types of steamers as well as sailing vessels. These were not borne on the lists, as is usual with us, but were nevertheless useful as school ships, store and coal hulks.

The discipline of the Peruvian navy was very lax, and drills were almost unknown. Peru had a naval school, but the important factor of practical exercises was entirely omitted from the course. Like Chile, Peru had no navy-yard, depending for repairs on private machine shops, of which there are a number at Callao, and on the works of the Pacific Steam Navigation Company. There is an iron floating dock at Callao, belonging to an English company, capable of taking up a 3,000-ton ship.

Peru depends on England, the United States, and Australia for her coal supply.

The uniform of the Peruvian navy has been modeled after the English, except that for the grades above lieutenant they have retained the shoulder-strap. The full dress of flag officers is also, very much more elaborate.

IV.

PREPARATIONS FOR WAR.

As soon as it was certain that Peru would fight, the Chilian Government began to prepare for war in earnest. Agents were sent to Europe to purchase arms, equipments, and military stores. A number of regiments were ordered to be raised, and were soon filled by volunteers. Several were recruited entirely from the miners who had been driven out of Chile. The regular regiments were filled to their war strength of about 1,200 men. To officer the new regiments officers were transferred from the regular service; the vacancies in the regular regiments and those which remained, after the transfers, in new regiments were filled from the non-commissioned ranks of the regulars and from suitable material in the volunteers. The most rigid discipline was enforced and the greater part of each day was spent in drilling. According to our views entirely too much time was devoted to mechanical precision and too little to skirmishing. Open-order fighting did not seem to form part of the system of tactics. The red and blue cloth clothing of the troops was supplemented by an excellent blouse and loose trowsers of brown hollands. A kepi of the same material replaced the cloth cap and heavy shako. Boots, of undressed, uncolored leather, well sewed and pegged, with broad thick soles and low heels, were adopted for foot wear. A flannel scarf and two pairs of woolen socks were issued to each man. The old-fashioned cartridge boxes were superseded, after the battle of Dolores, by broad canvas belts fitted with an upper and a lower row of small pockets, the whole contrivance containing 200 rounds of ammunition. The lower row was kept full on the march, the upper one being filled just before an action from the field reserve. The sword bayonet was attached to a leather belt. A large roomy canvas haversack, in which provisions, small articles, and, if necessary, ammunition, could be carried, was worn slung by a broad russet-leather adjustable shoulder-strap. Each man was provided with a half gallon tin canteen, cylindrical in shape; fitting over one end was a circular tin dish with a deep cylindrical rim. Fitting over the bottom and holding the dish to the body of the canteen was a semi-cylindrical drinking cup; this was held in place by two projecting lugs, which took the shoulder sling strap of russet leather. An extra pair of bootees, a suit of cloth clothes, and a poncho were issued, to be worn in a roll over the body. Some of the regiments were provided also with ulsters, made in various patterns of grayish or brownish material, Although these were not all exactly alike, they were very comfortable, serviceable, and did not look badly. For their cloth clothing some of the regiments had the old colors, but many of the new regiments were provided with blue, grey, or brown materials; one especially, the Chacabuco, was uniformed so nearly in the prevailing color of the soil of the coast that, when lying off Antofagasta, it was almost impossible to distinguish the regiment at drill on the hills behind the town. The average weight carried was 60 pounds. No regular wagon train was organized, but pack animals and pack-saddles in great quantities were provided.

The field ambulance corps was large and well manned and equipped. The following was the organization, modeled on that of the French army during the last war, and serving under the Geneva Cross:

The corps was directed by a surgeon-general and consisted of four ambulances, each directed by a chief surgeon. Each ambulance was subdivided into six sections, each consisting of a chief surgeon, four second surgeons, eight assistant surgeons, and twenty-four men. Each section was provided with 133 stretchers, a large number of medical canteens, and twelve large tents, capable of containing twelve men each. The stretchers were carried by the men and by mules; the tents in hospital wagons, which also carried the medicine and instrument chests.

The commissary department was administered by a commissary-general, assisted by divisional, brigade, and regimental commissaries. During peace the men live on their pay, their cooking and washing being done by their wives, who always accompanied the troops until the marked inconvenience of such a practice became evident to the commander-in-chief at Antofagasta; a regular commissariat was then organized. Rations are now issued and the men have coffee at daybreak, breakfast at 10 a. m.; and dinner at 5 p. m. Large soup kettles were carried by each regiment, in which the provisions were cooked over extemporized fire-places, a commissioned officer being present when the contents were issued.

The ration consisted of:

	Grams.
Dry beef	150
Beans	350
Mashed wheat	120
Rice (for officers)	120
Biscuit	200
Flour	200
Toasted wheat	200
Onions	50
Lard	50
Pepper	5
Salt	15
Potatoes	150
Sugar (brown)	25
Sugar (white, for officers)	25
Coffee	10

Marching ration:

	Grams.
Dry beef	460
Biscuit	460
Toasted wheat	200
Onions	100
Pepper	10

Two hundred and thirty grams of fresh beef may be substituted in place of the dry beef and beans.

Ration for animals: Grass, 9 kilograms; barley, 3 kilograms. When barley cannot be obtained, grass, 15 kilograms.

The organization of the troops was as follows:

Engineers (zapadores).—One regiment, recruited from the miners at Antofagasta, consisting of four brigades of two companies each, numbering in all about 1,200 men. The officers were generally engineers by profession. Arms, Comblain rifle and sword bayonet. No intrenching tool carried on the march; shovels, picks, and hatchets carried by pack animals.

Artillery.—Two regiments of three brigades each, each brigade consisting of two batteries, each battery of four or six guns and about 100 men. The guns were of many kinds; but the batteries consisted as nearly as possible of the same classes. The following were the kinds included: twelve 12-pounder 7.5 centimeter breech-loading Krupp rifles; seven 9-pounder 6.5 centimeter breech-loading Armstrong rifles; twenty three 6-pounder 7.5 centimeter breech-loading rifles, mountain Krupps; twelve 6-pounder 6 centimeter breech-loading rifles, mountain Krupps; four unknown; six long Gatlings, caliber .50.

The men were all armed with swords, and the higher numbers had Winchester repeating carbines and carried in action 80 rounds of ammunition. The carriages were some of wood and some of iron, but all were fitted with brakes.

The heavy guns were drawn by 8 horses each, and 20 spare horses were allowed to each battery; 8 of these were harnessed to the water wagons and 8 to the spare ammunition caissons. Each mountain gun and carriage had three mules and its ammunition four others. Each Gatling had four mules.

At the battle of Tacna four 6-pounder 6 centimeter breech-loading rifles, mountain Krupps, were captured and replaced the four unknown guns.

Cavalry.—The cavalry consisted of three regiments each of about 400 men, divided into four squadrons. The men were picked, and were tall and heavy, but seemed to be efficient in their work. The horses were solid and well built, about 15 hands high. A modification of the Mexican saddle, with a halter bridle, lasso, and single picket, was used. Besides being picketed, the horses are hobbled. The arms were a Winchester repeating rifle slung across the back, and a French cavalry saber.

Infantry.—The infantry was divided into regiments of eight companies each, the company numbering when full 150 men. The officers were a colonel, one lieutenant-colonel, one major, eight captains, eight lieutenants, sixteen sub-lieutenants, and one color lieutenant. Each regiment had a full band and each company its field music, consisting of buglers, half of whom were also drummers. These regiments were united in brigades of from three to five regiments, according to numerical strength; two brigades formed a division. To each division were attached two brigades of artillery and a regiment of cavalry. The men were armed with either Comblain or Gras rifles (improved Chassepot bolt-guns) and sword bayonets. Both guns require the same cartridge, about caliber .45, made at Santiago in a Government manufactory. The regiments were distinguished by the initial letter of their name on the cap, and a colored chevron on the arm. Each man carried a knife in his boot-leg, for eating purposes.

On account of the danger of injury to the arms of all kinds from blowing sand, breech mechanisms were carefully covered with leather aprons, and the muzzles were fitted with tompions. Many of the men further protected their arms (of which they were very fond, and which they kept in excellent condition) with cloth or baize covers. The scabbards of the cavalry and artillery were generally wound with strips of cloth, which served a double purpose by also reducing the noise.

Small national colors were carried by each regimental organization. The tents used were various in shape and size. Spare ammunition for the fighting line was carried on pack mules.

Of course all these details were not perfected at the very outset; but as it would be tiresome to follow them through their various stages, they have been collected here.

Besides putting her army in fighting trim, Chile increased her navy by repurchasing the corvette Abtao, by purchasing the fine screw steamer Amazonas for a transport, from the Pacific Steam Navigation Company, and by chartering the Rimac, Itata, Lamar, Limari, and Loa steamers of the Chilian Steam Navagation Company, and the Mathias Cousiño and other steamers of the Cousiño estate.

The upper spars of the Chilian vessels were sent on shore and the lower yards, if retained to serve as derricks, were cock-billed. The head booms were unrigged, and all but the standing bowsprits of the wooden vessels sent with the upper spars. From the very outset the Chilians showed their intention to carry on their operations under steam alone.

The crews of the ships were increased, plenty of material being at hand on account of the banishment of the Chilians from Peru and the consequent inability of the Pacific Steam Navigation Company to employ Chilian crews; not a few came direct from the Peruvian navy.

Many officers who had retired from active service in the navy and adopted other callings, or had taken service in the merchant marine, volunteered their services and were recommissioned. To this number were added officers of the merchant marine proper, especially those of the steamship line, who, by their knowledge of the coast, were eminently fitted to take part in the war. Those officers of the navy who were in foreign services also returned, bringing with them the very latest ideas from abroad.

Thus Chile was enabled to array a small but well-organized, well-constituted, and well-disciplined army and navy to cope with her numerically more powerful enemies.

In Bolivia a levy *en masse* was decreed, which, coupled with a general pardon to those opposed to the *régime* in power, brought a large number of men to the colors. The material of the rank and file was excellent, but there were no officers capable of reducing this raw material to a trained army. The recruits were principally Indians, who showed docility, endurance, and determination worthy of all praise. For long and toilsome marches these men have no superiors. Accustomed to perform long journeys, carrying heavy loads, and subsisting for days at a time on the mastication of the coca leaf, they were naturally fitted for the work in hand. But for modern war purposes the chief requisites could be imparted by instructors only, and these instructors seemed to be entirely wanting. To arm and equip these troops a forced loan was decreed and only partially raised. Several thousand Bolivian Indians, badly uniformed if uniformed at all, shod with sandals or barefoot, armed with the fire-arms of every period but the present, without commissariat, transport, or medical services, set out under General Daza to join the Peruvians at Tacna.

On the 26th of March, 1879, General Daza issued a decree offering letters of marque to any one who would attack the Chilian commerce and refuge to all privateersmen who would seize Chilian goods in whatever bottoms found. This call was not responded to, although agents were sent abroad. Most of the neutral Governments took active steps to oppose it.

Although the Chilians had accused the Peruvians of preparing for war, and had demanded that the preparations should cease, very little was actually done. The newspapers were clamorous for war. A large number of decrees were issued—one banishing every Chilian, including at first all women, even those married to foreigners and resident in Peru. This was, of course, modified, as the foreign ministers took the matter in hand. Very short time was allowed for these persons to leave the country. At some places on the coast it became necessary for the foreign men-of-war to lend their assistance in moving them. The raising of a large number of regiments was ordered.

The senior Peruvian naval officer afloat was Captain Miguel Grau, who was born in the northern city of Puira in 1834, educated at the nautical school of Paita, when that town was the headquarters of the whaling fleet. Was graduated with distinction, when he was sent to sea in a merchantman by his father. Returning from this cruise, he became a coast pilot, and in 1856 entered the navy as a sub-lieutenant. In 1863 he was promoted to the rank of lieutenant, and two years after to that of lieutenant-commander, passing shortly afterward to the grade of commander. In 1868 he was ordered to command the Huascar. In the election of 1873 he was chosen to represent the district of Paita in Congress. Here he remained until the war cloud burst, when he requested to be returned to his old command. Grau would have been an ornament to any service; a good seaman, an intelligent officer, a man of quiet, unassuming manners, a high-minded, brave, and honorable gentleman, he was beloved and respected by every one who came in contact with him. Through the exertions of Captain Grau, aided by Captain Moore, of the Independencia, the fleet was prepared for sea. The crews were filled up by transfers from the army and recruiting in Callao.

The fine steamer Oroya was purchased from the Pacific Steam Navigation Company, permissible probably as an offset for the purchase of the Amazonas from the same source by the Chilians.

The ships were divided into three divisions: The first, under Captain Grau, consisting of the Huascar (iron-clad), Independencia (iron-clad), Oroya (armed transport). The second, under Captain Carillo, consisting of the Manco Capac (iron-clad), Atahualpa (iron-clad), Chalaco (armed transport). The third or light division, under Captain Garcia y Garcia, consisted of the Union (corvette), Pilcomayo (corvette), Limoña (armed transport).

No steps were taken at first to erect new fortifications at Callao, nor even to improve those that already existed. The decrees ordering the organization of a large number of regiments resulted in bringing to Lima some thousands of Indians from the interior. Whilst in Chile drilling was going on on every side, in Peru there was an apparent lack of that important preparation for action. There was no organization beyond that of regiments. There was no commissariat; no artillery worthy of the name; no engineers, and no working general staff. The ambulance corps were in some cases mere holiday organizations. The regular army, 3,000 of which had been sent to Iquiqui, remained otherwise on a peace footing. Agents were sent abroad to buy arms, and soon began to forward Remington rifles, caliber .50, a large number of Peabody-Martini rifles bearing the Turkish stamp and with sights marked in Turkish characters, and repeating carbines of various manufactures, notably the Winchester, Henry, Spencer, and Peabody make. Some Gatling machine guns were also sent, but at first no artillery. The two mountain batteries of the regular army were armed, each, with 4 obsolete muzzle-loading 6-pounder rifles. To this number were added during the war about an hundred guns, mostly manufactured in Lima by inexperienced gun-makers. Among these were a number of 12-pounder and 6-pounder breech-loading White rifles. This gun was made of bronze, with an interrupted screw breech-plug. The projectiles were steel shell, with soft metal expanding rings, and a fuse of the maker's own invention. As is usual in bronze rifles the lands stripped after a few fires. Another variety was the Grieve 4½-pounder rifle, made from an ingot of steel bored out, with a wrought-iron trunnion band and reinforce band, both shrunk on. They were fitted with the wedge-breech. The projectiles were steel shell with percussion fuse; charge, eight ounces fine-grain powder; extreme range, 5,000 yards. Another class of small steel gun had a reinforce band of bronze shrunk on. It was impossible to ascertain how these worked. From Europe came later a few Krupps, Vavasseurs, and two Nordenfelt machine guns.

The men subsisted themselves, receiving a paper sol per day, which varied in value during the war from 40 to 7 cents. The soldiers were always accompanied by women and children. The uniform and equipment of the army were not improved during the war, and the arms, owing to want of care, became covered with rust and gummed with bad oil.

V.

FROM THE DECLARATION OF WAR, APRIL 2, 1879, TO THE NAVAL BATTLE OF IQUIQUI, MAY 21, 1879.

Whilst the Chilians and Bolivians were contending for the possession of the Atacama district, which resulted in the fight at Calama already described, the Peruvians sent a force of 3,000 regulars, under Colonel Manuel Velarde, to Iquiqui, where they were first placed under the command of Colonel Davila, the prefect, this officer being at the same time relieved of his political duties by General Lopez Lavalle. Later General José Buendia was sent to command the Army of the South, as it was called, Colonel Lopez being ordered to command the first or vanguardia division of that army. Although these troops were sent to Iquiqui, no attempts were made to fortify the town, whose only means of defense was a battery of four 9-pounder field-pieces. Several heavy guns were sent with the troops, but for some reason they were never mounted. Coincident with the declaration of war on April 2, the Chilians began to collect an army at Antofagasta, which was placed under the command of General Erasmo Escala.

On the 5th of April the Chilian squadron, under Rear-Admiral Rebolledo Williams, consisting of the Cochrane, Blanco, O'Higgins, Chacabuco, and Esmeralda, appeared off Iquiqui. The Chilian commander gave warning that all neutral vessels must leave the port before the 15th, when a regular blockade would be established.

On the 12th of April the Chilian corvette Magellanes, under Commander J. J. Latorre, on her way to join the squadron, met the Union and Pilcomayo, under Captain Garcia y Garcia, off Point Chipana, near the mouth of the river Loa; an action took place which lasted about two hours, at the end of which time the Magellanes, owing to her superior speed, succeeded in escaping. The Union was quite seriously injured. Owing to this injury and in order to increase her speed she returned to Callao, where she was immediately docked.

On April 15 some of the Chilian vessels visited the guano-loading ports of Huanillos and Pabellon de Pica, where they ordered off the vessels that were loading and destroyed the loading apparatus. The same day, a strict blockade having been declared, the last neutral vessels, two Americans, were assisted out of the port of Iquiqui by details of men from the United States ship Pensacola, which vessel had also assisted in the embarkation of nearly all the population of the place on board of steamers and sailing vessels. Most of these persons were Chilians.

On April 18 the Cochrane and Chacabuco appeared off Mollendo; the boat sent in to communicate was fired at, whereat the ships opened fire upon the railway station and upon the custom-house. No very serious damage was done.

On the same day the Chilians were off Pisagua. A large quantity of coal was stored here for the use of the railroad which was almost completed between this place and Iquiqui. As at Mollendo, the boats sent in to communicate and destroy the launches were fired upon and several of their crews were reported by the Chilians to have been killed. A heavy fire of guns and rockets was opened on the town, and a great part of it was destroyed by a conflagration caused by a rocket. During the bombardment the residence of the English consul was destroyed. The loss caused by the fire was estimated at $1,000,000, most of which unfortunately fell upon foreigners. A woman and a Chinaman were the only persons killed.

The squadron then returned to Iquiqui, from which place the Cochrane was sent to Valparaiso to be overhauled. An interesting fact connected with the blockade at Iquiqui was the difficulty experienced by the troops in obtaining fresh water. Before the war the supply was obtained in water boats from Arica, or by condensing. The failure of the first means caused the abandonment of almost all of the small towns, and at Iquiqui an order from the blockaders forbade the use of the condensers under a threat of bombardment. This could easily be enforced, as the smoke from the chimneys betrayed an infraction of the order. A case of this kind occurred on the 19th of April, in consequence of which fourteen heavy shell were thrown in the direction of the offending chimney, without doing serious damage.

During the night of May 16 President Prado, leaving the Government in charge of Vice-President La Puerta, left Callao in the Oroya, accompanied by the Independencia, Huascar, Limeña, and Chalaco. The Manco Capac and Atahualpa were to have gone, but at the last moment it was decided to leave them. The President was accompanied by a large staff and a body-guard of 50 young Peruvians, of good family, splendidly armed, equipped, and mounted. On board the transports and men-of-war were several regiments, a quantity of arms for the Bolivian contingent, a good supply of stores, and a large amount of money. It may be interesting to note here that although all movements on this coast have to be made by sea, the difficulties usually attending such transportation are greatly reduced by the continual fine weather, which admits of the men being very much crowded, and by the continual running of the steamers of the Pacific Steam Navigation Company, admissible by a clause in our treaty, as well as by a "most-favored-nation" clause in that with England. These steamers were made to transport most of the provisions for both armies, a fictitious or temporary consignee being all that was necessary.

This expedition having run well out to sea reached Arica in safety, where President Prado assumed the office of Supreme Director of the War, it having been arranged between the allies that the command should rest with the commander-in-chief of the army belonging to the country in which they were operating. General Daza had arrived at Tacna with about 4,000 of his men.

Peru was now receiving, by way of the Isthmus of Panama, the arms ordered from abroad. With them came a number of Lay torpedoes, accompanied by skilled machinists, and two Herreshoff torpedo-boats, shipped in sections and put together in Callao. One was ruined at the first trial; the other, after long practice and many failures, was driven up to a speed of about nine knots.

Having convoyed the transports to Arica and having landed the troops which they carried, the Huascar and Independencia left that place at 8 p. m. of the 20th for the south, news having reached them of the movement of the Chilian squadron to the north, and of the consequently unprotected state of the coast and weakness of the blockade at Iquiqui.

In the mean time Admiral Williams, having received information of the proposed movement of the Peruvian fleet from Callao and hoping to bring about a general action at sea, started north, May 16, with the Cochrane, Blanco, O'Higgins, Chacabuco, Magellanes, and Abtao, the latter filled with combustibles, it being intended to use her as a fireship. The Esmeralda and Covadonga, which on account of the bad condition of their engines would only have delayed the other ships, were left to enforce the blockade at Iquiqui. Running close along the shore in hopes of meeting the Peruvians, who, as we have stated, kept well out to sea, the Chilian squadron arrived off Callao during the night of May 21-22. A steam-launch was sent in to reconnoiter, and probably discovered the absence of the enemy. At sunrise the whole squadron was seen steaming in line ahead off the port, this evolution being continued until 11 a. m., when they left for the southward again.

It had been Admiral Williams's intention, if he found the Peruvian fleet still in Callao, to run the Abtao alongside of the Huascar, and, imitating Cochrane's brilliant exploit, set fire to her, then by the light of the conflagration attack the rest of the fleet with the rams and guns. The stay off Callao, after the discovery of the absence of the most effective part of the Peruvian fleet, if an attack was not intended on the monitors and town, cannot be accounted for, unless Admiral Williams was not willing to leave until he had satisfied himself of the departure of the iron-clads.

During the night of May 20-21 the Huascar, under Captain Grau, senior officer, and the Independencia, Capt. J. G. Moore, touched at Pisagua to make sure of the absence of the Chilian iron-clads. Being reassured they continued on, and at daylight on the morning of the 21st, were seen approaching Iquiqui.

As soon as Commander Arturo Prat, senior officer, commanding the Esmeralda, made out the enemy, he signaled to Commander Carlos Condell, commanding the Covadonga, to take position in his wake, and these two small vessels prepared for action. It was doubtless the purpose of Prat, from the first, to fight, though the disparity of force was so great. He could not escape on account of his low speed, but he would not have been much blamed by the world at large if he had destroyed his ships, surrendering himself and his crews, or if after a few shots he had surrendered all. But Prat was not the man to take advantage of either of these methods of saving life. Born April 3, 1848, he was still a very young commander. He had been a marked man in his service, having held positions of the greatest trust; by his conduct in the capture of the Covadonga and in quelling a serious mutiny on board the Peruvian corvette Union he had gained a reputation for gallantry; by being selected more than once as an instructor in gunnery at the naval school he had proved his theoretical proficiency in that all-important branch of study. Was this young senior officer fitted by his antecedents to surrender? The answer to this question is his conduct in the engagement which was about to take place—a fight that astonished the naval world; which established the precedent that, no matter what the odds be, vessels must be fought to the last, and which on account of the intelligence and intrepidity that characterized it, and on account of the harm that was actually done to the powerful opponent, deserves a whole page in the records of fame.

It was a curious combination of circumstances that brought Grau and Prat together in deadly combat, both to die, sword in hand, in the heat of combat, within a few feet of the same spot on the deck of the Huascar, each being at the time of his death the senior officer of an immensely inferior force contending nobly against great odds.

At 8 a. m., the Huascar fired a shot that struck between the two Chilian vessels, and the action immediately became general; the Huascar singling out the Esmeralda, and the Independencia the Covadonga. The Chilian transport Lamar, which was also in port when the enemy was sighted, was sent off to the southward and took no part in the fight. After the firing had been going on for an hour, at distances varying from two thousand yards to, perhaps, one thousand, the Covadonga steered to the south, the Independencia following her closely.

The Esmeralda remained in Iquiqui harbor, fighting the Huascar. By this time the Peruvian soldiers had dragged a field battery to the beach, and opened fire at distances not exceeding four or five hundred yards. Thus, with the 300-pounders of the Huascar on one side, and a field battery on the other, the Esmeralda was forced to abandon her position near the shore, which she had taken to avoid a ram attack from the enemy, and go farther out in the bay. The time when this occurred, and that at which the Huascar first rammed, has not been fixed satisfactorily; but it could not have been far from half past ten, two hours and a half after the beginning of the fight. It appears that Captain Grau was deterred from ramming by the fear of torpedoes, which he supposed were placed around the Esmeralda; and he rammed only when the latter vessel was driven from the place which she had first occupied, by the fire of the field battery on shore. The defense of the Chilian vessel would have lasted a much longer time if the fight had been decided entirely by the guns. The Huascar kept up a fire from all her guns for four hours, and during this time must have fired at least forty shots from her two 300-pounders; yet it is recorded that only one of these shots struck the enemy. This shot passed through the side, burst in the engine-room, and killed every one of the engineers, besides disabling the engine. The reply of the Esmeralda was most effective, as is testified by Captain Grau; but musketry and 40-pound shot are no match for 7-inch armor. Captain Grau is in error when he speaks of the mitrailleuse fire of the Chilians, in his report; neither the Esmeralda nor the Covadonga had machine guns of any kind. The Huascar had one long Gatling.

When the Esmeralda came out in the bay Captain Grau determined to ram her. In the first attempt, the Huascar, steaming about 8 knots and steering NE., struck the Esmeralda, nearly motionless and heading N., on the port quarter. The Huascar's engine was stopped when she was about one ship's length from her adversary. The blow was harmless. Captain Prat, followed by one man only, gallantly sprang on the forecastle, and, sword in hand, rushed aft on the port side of the deck, and was killed by a musket-ball at the foot of the turret. The command now devolved on Lieutenant Serrano. The Huascar backed off and made at the Esmeralda again, this time heading south; the Chilian vessel presented her bow; the Huascar's engines were stopped too soon, and she struck the starboard bow of the enemy, doing little or no damage. Again a boarding party, headed by the commanding officer, Lieutenant Serrano, leaped on the Huascar's deck, but only to be shot down. The third attempt of the Huascar was better conducted. The head of the Chilian vessel had fallen off to W., and Captain Grau, steering S., going full speed, and stopping his engines when 20 feet from the Esmeralda, struck his adversary squarely on the starboard beam. The Esmeralda sank with her colors flying and guns firing.

The Covadonga, meanwhile, was doing all that seamanship and courage could dictate to get away from her huge pursuer. She led along close to the shore, crossing shoal places, and actually, at times, almost in the breakers. The Independencia, with her raw, unskilled gunners, could not hit the little craft, though the vessels must have been within two hundred yards of each other several times. Captain Moore, fearing that he could never end the affair with his guns, determined to ram; this he tried three times, and failed to accomplish. The third attempt was made at Punta Grueso, at a time when the Covadonga was not one hundred yards from the beach and had actually touched on the reef. Steering about S.S.E., the Independencia aimed an oblique blow at the Covadonga's starboard quarter, and, missing her enemy, struck a rock and stuck fast. It appears from the reports of both captains, Moore and Condell, that the helm of the Peruvian ship was not ported early enough to prevent her going ashore, because a shot from one of the Covadonga's 70-pounders killed her helmsman. The only steering-wheel of the Independencia was the ordinary one on deck.

It must have been 11.45 a. m. when the Independencia struck. Captain Condell, seeing at once the state of affairs, turned his vessel, and, passing along the starboard side of the enemy, coolly took his position astern of him and began to fire. It has been asserted that the Independencia's ensign was hauled down and a flag of truce hoisted, on account of the deliberate fire of the enemy and her inability to return it, having fallen over on her starboard side, and her lower part having filled with water. To add to the discomfiture of those on board, a shell from the Covadonga, or an accident, set fire to the after part of the vessel.

Immediately after the surrender of the Independencia, and before she was taken possession of, the Huascar, which, having sunk the Esmeralda at 12.10 p. m., had remained to pick up the survivors of her crew, came around the western end of the island which forms the south side of Iquiqui Bay. She was about 10 miles off, and the Covadonga, having evidently disposed of the Independencia, was steaming rapidly away. The Huascar, after speaking her stranded consort to ascertain whether there was any immediate danger to the life of the crew, resumed her pursuit of the Covadonga. This pursuit lasted until dark, when Captain Grau, seeing that there were still 10 miles between him and the chase, and probably uneasy about the enemy's iron-clads, whose position was unknown to him, gave up the pursuit and returned to the Independencia. This vessel it was clearly impossible to save, and she was set on fire and burned.

Nothing could have been better than Prat's plan of action. First remaining stationary in a corner between the island and the shore, he limited the field of his adversary's maneuvers to ram, conveying also the idea that he was protected by those terrors of modern naval warfare, torpedoes. This impression was rendered doubly certain in Captain Grau's mind by the report of the Peruvian captain of the Port of Iquiqui, who managed to get aboard the Huascar in his boat. Again, by assuming this position, he reduced Grau to the painful necessity of sending his shell, at moderately short range, directly towards the town which was occupied by his own countrymen. When forced by the fire of the shore guns, more dangerous, at that short range, against his wooden walls than the 300-pounders of the iron-clad, he hugged the shore as closely as possible, keeping up a heavy, well-directed fire from his guns of all kinds, how well-directed the condition of the Huascar after the fight clearly showed. One shot entered the turret through one of its ports, and after balloting about considerably, came to rest without injuring any one. Had this been a shell, it might have entailed considerable loss. Other shots cut the tripod foremast nearly away; so insecure did it become that Captain Grau feared that it would fall, in which case it would probably jam the turret. When the ramming began Prat called away his boarders, and, as already stated, actually succeeded, with one sergeant of marines, in reaching the enemy's deck. Had the contact been of longer duration he would have succeeded, probably, in transferring his crew to the decks of the Huascar with a a very fair chance, according to Captain Grau himself, of capturing the vessel, as the crew was, with very few exceptions, very much demoralized. Serrano's attempt failed from the same cause. When the Huascar did finally succeed in sinking the Esmeralda, which was then little more than a stationary target, she injured her own bow so severely that extensive repairs were necessary. The musketry fire of the Esmeralda was so well sustained that it was thought that she was provided with machine guns.

Condell could not have done better with his little ship. That he followed the correct tactics in keeping close to the shore was proved by the results. His artillery fire, which was continued throughout the chase, was so excellent that he dismounted the heavy bow pivot of the Independencia before it had succeeded in sending more than one shot into him. What the effect would have been if this had not occurred may be imagined from the fact that this shot entered the starboard quarter, raked the whole length of the ship, and passed out on the port bow. The other two guns, being protected by iron plating, continued to fire with but moderate results, owing to the want of training of the guns' crews. The small-arm fire of the Covadonga kept the enemy's crew below, and killed the three helmsmen at the critical moment, according to Captain Moore, who, like Captain Grau, mistook it for machine-gun fire.

It was thus that Captain Prat's speech made to his officers and crew before the fight was carried out in its fullest details. Had the results of the action been different, it might have passed for bombast; as it is, it becomes a fitting text for the naval students of the future:

"Children, the odds are against us; our flag has never been lowered in the presence of the enemy; I hope that it will not be to-day. As long as I live that flag shall fly in its place, and if I die, my officers will know how to do their duty."

Captain Moore was placed under arrest and kept a close prisoner on the Moro at Arica. The two 150-pounders of the Independencia were afterwards raised by the Peruvians and taken to Iquiqui.

This action, of course, raised the blockade of Iquiqui, and about four thousand troops, Bolivians and Peruvians, were thrown into the place, which was visited also by General Prado.

The Huascar was considerably injured in the action, her tripod mast was so much damaged that it had to be removed on her return to Callao, her bow leaked from broken plates, and her turret was slightly out of line. She continued her cruise, however, to the southward. At Antofagasta she exchanged shots with the Covadonga, that lay inside of the reef, and was supported by three 150-pounders mounted in sand batteries along the face of the town. During this action the Huascar was struck by a 150-pounder projectile under her counter, close to the water-line. This shot penetrated the armor, although it struck sideways. The Huascar grappled and cut the submarine cable, thus temporarily severing the communication between that place and Valparaiso.

The Huascar then turned north. Off Huanillos, at 5.50 a. m., June 3, she sighted two vessels, which in the haze were supposed to be the O'Higgins and Chacabuco. She stood towards them, and when about 5 miles distant discovered that she had to deal with the Blanco and Magellanes. These vessels gave chase. On account of the bad quality of the coal taken at Pacocha and Pisagua the Huascar at first could make only about 9 knots, but after a time succeeded in increasing her speed, and after 18 hours of hard running managed to escape. A few shots were exchanged, but without important results.

On June 7th the Huascar reached Callao, where she was received with great enthusiasm; her commander was fêted. A unanimous vote of Congress promoted him to the grade of rear-admiral, but at his own request he was allowed to retain his old command, as he realized that there was no one to replace him in that all-important position.

Admiral Grau now insisted upon being furnished with a new crew, or at least with some men on whom he could rely as gunners and helmsmen. These were easily picked up among the sailor boarding-houses, as so many foreign merchants ships were out of employment on account of the almost entire cessation of the nitrate and guano trades. Soon afterward the unprecedented demand of the year for grain-ships at San Francisco took most of these vessels north. The trade of the whole Peruvian coast was destroyed. Among the new men shipped were several regularly trained gunners.

Besides organizing his new crew, Grau devoted himself to superintending the repairs of his ship. The foremast was removed, the main, which was used for signals and as a post for a lookout, was left standing, the main-top, fitted with an iron screen, was arranged as a post for a Gatling and riflemen in action.

VI.

FROM THE RE-ESTABLISHMENT OF THE BLOCKADE OF IQUIQUI TO THE BATTLE OF ANGAMOS, OCTOBER 8, 1879.

On the return of the Chilian squadron from Callao, the blockade of Iquiqui was re-established under Captain Simpson, of the Cochrane. Admiral Williams went to Valparaiso in the Blanco. Great dissatisfaction was expressed at the manner in which he had conducted affairs, and it was determined to relieve him from command. Captain Salamanca, his chief of staff, was ordered to Coquimbo as captain of the port, and Captain Simpson, his second in command, was shortly afterwards relieved by Captain Latorre, of the Magellanes. Simpson was ordered to duty with the army at Antofagasta. Commodore Galvarino Riveros was placed in command of the squadron with Lieutenant-Commander Castillo as chief of staff.

The O'Higgins and Chacabuco were refitted and were provided with new boilers at Valparaiso, advantage being taken of the season of northers, when it was reasonable to expect that the Peruvians would not venture to risk their reduced force on the Chilian coast. The organization of the army at Antofagasta was pushed ahead with great activity.

About this time a torpedo launch that had been fitted out by the Peruvians was captured near Pisagua.

The army of Tarapaca, under General Buendia, with Colonel Granier, of the Bolivian army, at Pisagua, now numbered about ten thousand men. For some unaccountable reason, Iquiqui was closely blockaded, while Pisagua, its side door, was left open so that through it the Peruvians were able to receive re-enforcements and provisions. Amongst the articles said to have been sent were three Lay torpedoes and an expert to handle them.

After being repaired and remanned the Huascar started on a second raid to the southward. On July 9 she arrived at Arica, where the admiral communicated with the director of the war, from whom he received orders to proceed south, and inflict as much damage as possible in capturing or destroying the enemy's transports and smaller vessels, but on no account to risk a combat with superior or even equal forces. He was also informed that it was the custom of the blockaders to get under way during the night and run well out to sea, as a precaution against torpedoes, of whose existence in Iquiqui they had become aware.

Leaving Arica, Grau ran into the Bay of Iquiqui the same night, and having communicated with General Buendia, started out again, when he discovered the transport Cousiño. He forced this vessel to surrender, and was about to take possession of her when he discovered a vessel steaming towards him. At first he thought it was the Cochrane, but a closer approach revealed the Magellanes. The Huascar headed towards her, and, at a distance of three hundred yards, fired a 300-pounder, at the same time opening a heavy fire of small-arms and machine guns. The Magellanes returned a stand of grape from her 64-pounder, and commenced a well-sustained fusillade, it being impossible to fire again with the great guns, as they could not be brought to bear. The Huascar made two attempts to ram, that were evaded by her lively antagonist. She then took her station at a distance of 100 yards from the starboard side of the latter and continued firing. This maneuver brought her within range of the 115-pounder of the Magellanes, one shot from which was fired, but without serious effect, although

Commander Latorre claims to have pierced the iron-clad at the water line. The Huascar turned and made another ram attack, coming perpendicularly to the enemy and aiming amidships; by a dash ahead this was avoided. A fourth attempt was made to ram, bow to bow, but with no better success. The Huascar had now fired six 300-pounder projectiles, the Magellanes one 115-pounder, one 64-pounder stand of grape, six 20-pounder shell, one 20-pounder grape, 2,400 small-arm cartridges, and 360 Adams revolver cartridges, and, with the exception of a considerable cutting up of rigging, boats, &c., and three men slightly wounded, the results were *nil*. The firing brought the Cochrane on the ground, and caused the Huascar, in obedience to the instructions received by her commander, to leave after a short running fight. It was after this fight that Captain Simpson was relieved of the command of the Cochrane by Captain Latorre.

The Chilians now changed their tactics and remained at anchor during the night. On the night of July 16 the lookouts on board the Cochrane reported an object in the water near the ship, that was supposed to be a Lay torpedo. Fire was immediately opened on it, and shortly afterwards forty shell were thrown into the town; a number of people, non-combatants and others, were killed, and some property destroyed.

On the 17th of July the Huascar again left Arica for the south, the Union accompanying her. They visited the ports of Caldera, Cavrigal, Bajo, and Pan de Azucar, destroying the launches used for landing, and capturing two merchantmen loaded with coal and copper. On the 26th the Huascar captured the large transport Rimac, that was conveying stores and a fine battalion of cavalry—the Yungay, Colonel Bulnes—to Antofagasta. Among the stores captured was a large supply of water-skins, intended for carrying water on a march that was then talked of from Antofagasta across the desert of Atacama to Iquiqui. Besides these valuable captures the Huascar had succeeded in making herself greatly feared, although Grau had not committed a single illegal or cruel act. His expeditions had caused Chile to spend large amounts in fortifying her ports, had rendered her trade uncertain, and had stopped the transportation of troops and stores without armed escorts.

The officers captured in the Rimac, together with those of the Esmeralda, were sent to Callao in the Pilcomayo and thence across the mountains to Tarma, where they were afterwards joined by the cavalrymen.

About this time the first actual improvements were made in the fortifications of Callao. A sunken battery was constructed on the long cobble point known as the Whale's Back. In this were mounted two 20-inch 1,000-pounder smooth-bore muzzle-loading guns—one a Rodman, the other a Dahlgren. Several heavy guns were also added to the batteries north of the town. Ancon, a landing place north of Callao, and Chorillos, to the south, were also slightly fortified.

The Huascar, still raiding in the south, entered the port of Caldera and almost captured the transport Lamar, which was saved only by being hauled into very shoal water behind the mole.

Amongst the articles captured in the Rimac was the official correspondence of the Government, from which it was learned that the Chilians expected two cargoes of arms from Europe by way of the Straits. The Union, under Captain Garcia y Garcia, was therefore dispatched to those waters, reaching Punta Arenas, the Chilian settlement in the Straits, August 18, just after the first cargo had passed through. The Union was coaled and provisioned, no resistance being made by the governor with his little guard of forty soldiers. The governor, it is said, assured Captain Garcia that both cargoes had passed, and sent him off in pursuit just as the second vessel was entering from the Atlantic. Two Chilian ships were sent down after the Union, but missed her.

Great dissatisfaction was now expressed in Chile in regard to the conduct of the war. The press began to cry loudly for change, for an advance of the army, for energetic movements by the navy to stop the successful career of the Huascar; for anything, in fact, which can usually be done better on paper than on the face of the globe. The people, excited by the press, began to give vent to their pent-up feelings in meetings, some of which bore a very close resemblance to mobs. The Government issued several decrees, abandoned the blockade of Iquiqui, brought all the vessels that could be spared from the protection of Antofagasta to Valparaiso for repairs; superseded Captain Simpson in command of the Cochrane by Captain Latorre, who was the hero of the hour, on account of his able management of the Magellanes; appointed Don Rafael Sotomayor minister of war, and sent him to Antofagasta to superintend matters.

On the 1st of August the monitor Manco Capac, convoyed by the Oroya, went from Callao to Arica. This place, which had become the headquarters of the allied army, was situated on the sea-shore, just north of a high bluff called the Moro, three sides of which were almost perpendicular; the fourth sloped inland. The crown of this bluff had been strongly fortified, and a semicircle of forts protected the town and the land face of the bluff. The monitor was needed to complete the circle of defense.

The Huascar had gone south again, having stopped at Iquiqui, now open, where she took on board two of the Lay torpedoes and an operator. She next appeared off Antofagasta, on the night of August 27. It is said that information of the absence of the iron-clads (which were at Valparaiso repairing) was given by a man whom she took out of the Pacific Steam Navigation Company's steamer Ilo, to the northward of the place. This person had embarked at Iquiqui as a through passenger to Montevideo. The following account of what next happened is generally accepted, but I have been unable to verify it to my entire satisfaction, owing to the unusual reticence of the official eye-witnesses. The

Huascar approached the Abtao, which lay at anchor off the reef, to a distance of 200 yards. This distance had been selected by the expert, although the admiral offered to place his vessel nearer. One of the torpedoes was then launched from the deck, and had proceeded some distance on its course, when it began to turn to port, making a half circle in that direction, and coming back towards the vessel. Efforts were made to stop it, but nothing but a reduction in speed was effected. Lieutenant Diez Canseco, appreciating the danger to which all were exposed, jumped overboard and caused the torpedo to deviate from its dangerous course. This trial thoroughly disgusted Grau with this system of torpedoes, and, on his return to Iquiqui, he had them landed and buried in the cemetery, where they were resurrected by the Chilians some months afterward.

The next day at 11 a. m. the Huascar, again ran in and engaged the shore batteries and corvettes Magellanes and Abtao, severely damaging the latter vessel, besides killing and wounding about 20 of her crew.

The Huascar was struck by a 150-pounder shell, that passed through her smoke-stack on the starboard side, and descending passed out through the smoke-stack and coaming of the fire-room hatch, about eighteen inches from the deck, on the other side, killing the lieutenant commanding the quarter-deck division of guns, who happened to be behind the smoke-stack at the time, wounding the ship's bugler, and, glancing on the water-way, passed overboard without exploding. Had this shot been a little lower it would have passed through the base of the stack, thence under the armored deck into the port boilers, there being no bomb-proof grating to stop it. A 300-pounder common shell, English service percussion fuse, struck the Abtao just at the end of its range of three thousand yards. The Abtao was at anchor without steam, and at the time heeled towards the Huascar. This shell came in on the starboard side, traversed the iron mainmast, struck the deck on the port side abreast the engine-room hatch and exploded, damaging the mainmast and bulwarks, tearing a hole in the composite deck about four by six feet, twisting the iron deck-beams, pieces of the shell breaking up the engine-room gallery plating and passing into the coal-bunkers, the coal in which saved the bottom of the ship. The chief engineer, who was on the spar-deck, and five men were killed. One of the latter had his head taken entirely off by the barrel of his own rifle, which he had slung across his back diagonally, a piece striking the muzzle, which projected above his right shoulder, his back being towards the enemy. Another similar projectile, fired in the same round a minute afterwards, glanced on the bridge-rail very close to the commanding officer, passed through the bridge-frame and ladder, went through the smoke-stack, struck a cavil-plate in the port water-way, and exploded, bulging out the side, and damaging the bulwarks and deck. This shot killed eight men. Both of these fires were remarkable for range and accuracy, and for the perfect action of the fuses used.

After leaving Antofagasta, the Huascar visited Taltal, Tocapilla, and Mejillones de Bolivia, capturing and destroying hulks and launches. She then returned north to Arica.

The two vessels that were loaded with arms and munitions and had escaped from the Union, arrived safely at Valparaiso, and their cargoes served to equip a new levy of 3,000 men who were already in a good state of discipline. Twelve men-of-war and transports left Valparaiso on the 20th of September for Antofagasta.

On the 1st of October, the Cochrane having been put in complete repair, the Chilian squadron, consisting of the Blanco, flagship of Commodore Riveros, the Cochrane, the O'Higgins, and Covadonga, and the transports Loa, Mathias Cousiño went north toward Arica. The Cousiño on approaching Arica, took in tow the steam launches of the two iron-clads rigged for torpedo service. A delay occurred in hoisting out the Blanco's boat, one of the pennants carried away, dropping and seriously injuring it. This caused the attack to be delayed twenty-four hours. At 3 o'clock on the morning of the 4th, the Cousiño having reached what was supposed to be a short distance from the port, the boats started on their mission to destroy the Huascar. On account of a miscalculation of the distance, they failed to arrive off the port until broad daylight; this, and the absence of the Peruvian iron-clad caused the attack to be relinquished. From some fishermen Commodore Riveros learned that the Huascar and Union had started on another raid to the southward. A council of war was called, and the question whether it were better to remain, bombard the defenses and sink the Manco Capac at the risk of injuries to their own ships and without a landing force to follow up their probable success, or to go south and attempt to capture the Huascar, was decided in favor of the second proposition.

The Huascar had been sent south with the Union on her fourth raid by order of General Prado, and against the advice of Admiral Grau. The latter asserted that his ship's bottom was exceedingly foul, and that her speed had been impaired by long, active service. He urged that he should be allowed to go to Callao, where the only means of making the necessary repairs existed, as he considered his vessel of too great value, in the present reduced state of the navy, to be needlessly risked. Other councils prevailed, however, and Peru's only hope started south September 30th, with her brave commander, the latter never to return, the former to add to the already superior strength of the enemy.

At about 2 o'clock on the morning of October 5, the Huascar and Union, having escorted the Rimac with a body of troops under General Bustamente to Iquiqui, appeared off the harbor of Coquimbo. The handling of these two vessels on this occasion was most admirable. Perfect quiet reigned in both, and, although they passed within a cable's length of the Pensacola, the only sound heard was a whispered order, in English, to "Go ahead slow." Captain Garcia y Garcia, the commander of the Union, has since said that great trouble was experienced in controlling the steam on board his vessel to prevent the necessity of blowing off. Not a shot was fired from the shore-batteries, which had been constructed at great expense, and were armed with guns at least one of which could have pierced the Huascar's armor. After cruising about the harbor, finding no transports, and not being able to draw the fires of the batteries, the two vessels went south around the point at a little after 3 a. m. All the next day they kept in sight to the southward of the port, managing to intercept two mail steamers, from which they learned of the Chilian move to the northward. During the 6th and 7th the Peruvians moved up the coast, and, although Admiral Grau's orders were, not to approach nearer than 70 miles to Antofagasta, where the Chilian squadron was supposed to be when he left Arica, he determined, on the strength of his later information, to look in at that place, especially as it had been reported to him that the Cochrane had broken down and was not able to accompany the squadron, as she could not use her engines. This fact, which was true, had been remedied and she had pursued her course. Leaving the Union on lookout near Point Tetas, the Huascar ran in towards the anchorage off Antofagasta at about 1.30 on the morning of October 8. Finding nothing to interest her there, she stood out and rejoined the Union at 3.15. Both vessels now stood round Point Tetas and headed north. A few minutes afterwards they made the smoke of three vessels coming along the coast, steering south, about 6 miles distant. These were soon after recognized as vessels of war, and the course, at 3.30, changed to southwest.

The Chilian squadron at Mejillones having coaled, put to sea during the night of the 7th in two divisions; the first, under Commodore Riveros, consisted of the slower vessels, Blanco, Covadonga, and Mathias Cousiño, left at about 10 p. m., and steered down the coast towards Antofagasta; the second, under Commander Latorre, consisted of the Cochrane, O'Higgins, and Loa, left at about 1 a. m. of the 8th, with orders to cruise 25 miles on and off Point Angamos. This was done in accordance with telegraphic instructions from the director of the war, and differed slightly from the original plan of the commodore, who intended to have moved south along the coast in similar divisions, the first division skirting the coast and looking in at the bays, while the second stood in the same direction but farther off shore, and about 40 miles on the starboard quarter of the first. Either of these plans would probably have entailed the same results. Thus it was that, at 3.30 on the morning of October 8, the weather being fine and clear, the lookout in the Blanco's top reported the smoke of two vessels approaching from under Point Tetas, distant about 6 miles. At daylight the enemies recognized each other. The Husacar ran for an hour to the southwest at full speed, making about 10¾ knots with sixty revolutions and an average pressure of 25.5 pounds of steam, the Blanco and Covadonga following, making about 7½ knots. The Mathias Cou siño was sent in towards Antofagasta, but later turned to the northward and followed her consorts. Commodore Riveros saw immediately that the chase was hopeless; still, on the chance of an accident to the machinery of the Huascar or her consort, or of their turning to the northward and being cut off by the second division, he determined to continue it.

It has been asked, and with good reason, whether the results of the battle might not have been different had the Peruvian ships engaged the Chilians at this time. It is true that the Union was a much more powerful vessel than the Covadonga, and that both she and the Huascar had a great advantage in speed. When, however, we consider that the admiral's orders were very explicit, and wisely so, that he should run no risks with his ships, as the loss of the Huascar would give the Chilians the command of the sea, it does not seem strange that he should have attempted to escape. Admiral Grau, finding that he was rapidly distancing his pursuers, turned to the northward at about 5.40, and eased his engines by reducing the revolutions to fifty-three. Having been on deck all night, he now lay down for some much needed rest. At about 7.15 smoke was seen, from the Huascar, on the horizon to the northwest, and at 7.30 she having stood slightly to the westward to reconnoiter, the Cochrane and her consorts were recognized. The Huascar was seen at about the same time from the Cochrane's top, and the Loa was sent to reconnoiter. Admiral Grau, who had now come on deck, probably felt confident that he could elude the Cochrane, as her speed, according to the latest information in his possession, was only eight knots, and stood for a short time towards the Loa. Finding, however, that the Cochrane was changing her bearings more rapidly than he had anticipated, he stood more to the east, and ordered full speed. The Union which had remained on the Huascar's port quarter, now, at about 7.45, crossed her stern and passed to starboard of her at full speed. From this moment this vessel, it is alleged, by order of the admiral, made the best of her way to Arica, followed until dark by the O'Higgins and Loa. The conduct of these three commanding officers has been much commented upon; the first for not engaging, the others for not continuing the pursuit. The three iron-clads were now about eight thousand yards distant from each other. Grau saw that his only chance of escape lay in his speed. At 9.10, as the Cochrane had approached to within less than four thousand yards, and it was evident that she could cross his bows, he ordered the crew to quarters, and shortly afterward entered his conning-tower alone. In going to quarters an accident occurred in shifting the lead from the ordinary steering-wheel under the poop to the fighting one in the turret-chamber under the conning-tower. This caused the Huascar to yaw considerably whilst a makeshift tackle was being rigged. At 9.25 the Cochrane, being about three thousand yards distant, the Huascar opened fire with her turret-guns. The second shot, ricocheting ahead of the Cochrane, entered her unarmored bows, and after smashing the galley and causing some slight damage fell on deck without exploding. At this time the Blanco was about six miles astern. The Cochrane did not answer these shots but stood on until within two thousand yards, when she opened fire. One of her first shots penetrated the Huascar's armor on the port side and exploding entered the turret-chamber, where it set fire to the light wood-work, killed and wounded twelve men, some of whom were at the winches used to revolve the turret, and drove its own fragments and *débris* of all kinds under the turret-trucks, which it jammed for the time being. A 10-inch 300-pounder Palliser chilled shell from the Huascar, fired at a range of six hundred yards, struck the Cochrane's starboard side-armor at an angle of thirty degrees. The plate, which was six inches thick, was indented or scored out to a depth of three inches, the bolts were moved, and the backing was forced in; a beam was also broken. The shell probably broke up.

At 9.40 the Huascar stood a little to port with the intention of ramming the Cochrane, but the latter prevented this by turning an equal amount to port and steering a parallel course. At 9.45 the conning-tower was struck by a shell, which exploded in it, shattering it very much and blowing Admiral Grau to pieces—only one foot and a few fragments being found. Admiral Grau usually directed the movements of his vessel with his head and shoulders out of the top of the tower; the shell, therefore, must have hit him at about the waist. The concussion from this shot caused the death of Lieutenant Diego Ferré, the admiral's aide, who was at the fighting-wheel, separated from the conning-tower by a light wooden grating only. This officer's body was mistaken for that of his commander, and caused the erroneous statements which appeared at the time of the combat. No wounds were found on Lieutenant Ferré's body. Part of this shot also disabled the fighting-wheel, and the vessel turned to starboard and ran to the eastward until the damage having been repaired she was again headed north. About this time a shell penetrated the armor of the turret (now trained on the port quarter) in its thickest part to the left of the port of the right gun, killing and disabling most of the guns' crews. Among the former were the two gun-captains, and among the latter Commander Meliton Carbajal, chief of staff, who had come to inform the second in command, Commander Elias Aguirre, that he was now in command. This shot furnishes the data for the killing effect of the projectile fired experimentally at the Glatton some years ago, which by a curious coincidence struck exactly the same part of the turret. Relief crews were sent to the guns, but the firing became very wild, as the men were comparatively inexperienced. The right gun had been disabled by the shot above mentioned, which bent the right compressor and cap-square. Lieutenant Rodriguez while looking out of one of the gun-ports had his head taken off. An eye-witness reports that the native part of the crew was much demoralized by the loss of their commander. The cabin and wardroom were full of men and officers, some wounded and many refugees from the upper deck, from which every one had been driven by the Nordenfelt and small-arm fire of the enemy.

The Cochrane now attempted to ram, coming at right angles to her adversary, firing her starboard bow gun at two hundred yards; the center gun missed fire. She missed the Huascar and passed about five yards astern of her. A shot from one of the Cochrane's port guns pierced the armor of her opponent on the starboard quarter, exploding and doing much damage, including carrying away the iron tiller-block, which served as a lead for both ordinary and fighting wheel ropes. The Huascar now again headed to the eastward. A shell pierced the armor abreast the engine-room, covering the engines with *débris*, and killing and wounding several persons in the engine-room gallery. Among the latter were Surgeon Tavara and Mr. Griffiths, the master of the schooner Coquimbo, captured a few days before, and whose crew were forced to render service during the action. The relieving-tackles, which had a very bad lead behind the transoms in the admiral's cabin, were now manned. The steering was very uncertain, as Commander Aguirre had to conn the vessel from one of the lookout hoods of the turret, and the word had to be passed clear aft on the lower deck to the men at the relieving tackles. The Cochrane again attempted to ram the Huascar, firing her starboard bow gun as before at two hundred yards, and coming on at right angles with the center guns trained abeam with three degrees depression. She again missed her blow, and passed astern. The center gun was being loaded at this time.

It was now about 10.10, and the Blanco arrived on the scene of action, passing between the Huascar and the Cochrane just as the latter was preparing to ram a third time. The Cochrane, to avoid the imminent danger in which she was placed by her consort's ram, was forced to turn to port and then to the northward, increasing her distance to twelve hundred yards. The Huascar turned to starboard and headed for the Blanco with the intention of ramming her, at the same time firing some ineffectual shots in her direction. The Blanco sheered to starboard also, and passing at about twenty-five yards' distance, poured a broadside into her stern, which killed or wounded all of the men at the relieving-tackles, and also many of the wounded and others assembled in the officers' quarters. The wounded were now removed to the coal-bunkers and store-rooms. The Huascar now stood to the westward.

On account of the number of shots which had traversed the smoke-stack, driving down soot, *débris*, and smoke into the fire-room, it was impossible to see the gauges. The water fell too low in one of the boilers, which allowed the tubes to be burned through, and caused a great escape of steam. This led the Chilians to believe that they had struck one of the boilers. The small-arm fire at some previous time killed and disabled three out of the four men stationed at the Gatling gun in the Huascar's top, although protected by a boiler-iron screen. The fourth man went below. This must have been done by the small-arm men in the Chilian tops; the latter were higher than that of the Huascar, which had no top covering or hood. The breast-high shield bore no evidence of having been penetrated from below. At 10.25 the Huascar's colors were shot away at the flag-staff, and for some moments she was supposed to have surrendered, and all firing ceased. A loader at one of the guns went aft and hoisted another flag at the gaff. A shot about this time penetrated the turret of the Huascar, killing or mortally wounding every man in it, including Commander Aguirre. Some idea of the terrible effects of this shot may be drawn from the fact that when this officer's body was found and identified, all the upper part of the head was gone, the lower jaw only remaining, four wounds on the right leg, a cut across the stomach, and six body wounds; the right shoulder and arm had disappeared entirely. He was standing at the time to the left and rear of the left gun, with his head in the sighting-hood. Lieutenant Palacios was terribly wounded by this shot. At Commander Latorre's urgent request Palacios was sent on board the next northern-bound mail steamer, but died before reaching Lima.

The command had devolved upon the fourth officer, Lieutenant Pedro Garezon. The vessel was almost unmanageable and on fire in several places; still the engines were kept going, and the left turret gun was fired occasionally. The Cochrane now returned and again tried to ram; she was only prevented from doing so by the chance movements of the Huascar. Both Chilian ships now followed the Huascar, using the bow and center guns, accompanied by an unceasing shower of small-arm and machine-gun projectiles. The Cochrane was struck during the action, probably when she turned off to give place to the Blanco, by a shell which entered her unarmored stern and caused considerable damage, wounding ten men, of whom two afterwards died. The Covadonga now came up and succeeded in putting herself on record by firing one gun. Lieutenant Garezon, after calling a council of surviving officers, sent Sub-Lieutenant Ricardo Herrera to the chief engineer with orders to attempt to sink the vessel by opening her valves. Chief Engineer Mac-Mahon and his assistants succeeded in partially accomplishing this by opening the circulating-valves of the condensers, to do which they had to stop the engines. They were at work on the bonnet of the main injection-valve when Lieutenant Simpson of the Cochrane interfered, revolver in hand. While this was going on below some of the men forward crawled up through the fore-hatch and waved towels and handkerchiefs, seeing which the Chilians ceased firing. The flag was then hauled down. As the Huascar's engines did not stop at first, they were going to reopen fire when she became motionless, probably for the reason already stated. She was immediately boarded by boats from the Cochrane, under Lieutenant Simpson, and from the Blanco, under Lieutenant-Commander Castillo, chief of staff to the commodore; with them came surgeons and engineers.

The Chilian officers on taking possession found from three to four feet of water in the hold. Some of the holes made in the sides by the projectiles were nearly awash, and in a few more minutes the vessel would have sunk. She was also found on fire in several places, especially over the magazines forward. Fortunately the sea was smooth, and the valves being closed, the pumps were started, the ship freed from water, and the fire extinguished. The wounded and prisoners were transferred to the Chilian ships. The Huascar's engines had received no damage, and three out of four of the boilers were in condition to be used; therefore with very little assistance she was enabled to go into the port of Mejillones during the afternoon, and in two days, her shot-holes having been temporarily stopped and steering gear repaired, she started in charge of a prize crew under Lieutenant Peña, the executive officer of the Blanco, for Valparaiso, where she was completely overhauled. Her plates which had been damaged were either replaced by some which had been brought from England to plate the Chacabuco and O'Higgins, or by plugging with masses of wrought iron hammered in. On the 8th of December she was again ready for active service.

The scene on board the Huascar when boarded was terrible. There was hardly a square yard of her upper works that did not bear marks of having been struck with some species of projectile. Her smoke-stack and conning tower were nearly destroyed, her boats gone, and davits either entirely carried away or bent out of all shape. Her mast was riddled and port chain-plates carried away, but, strange to say, no rigging was cut. The bulwarks, poop, forecastle, and hatch-coamings were much injured. The capstan was struck and knocked overboard by a shot. The Chilian fire must have been extremely accurate, a fact which is not surprising, as the Huascar was reduced during the latter part of the fight—in fact, from the time the Cochrane took up her position on her quarter—to a little more than an armored target. Below, the scene was much more terrible. Everywhere was death and destruction caused by the enemy's large shells. Eighteen bodies were taken out of the cabin, and the turret was full of remains of the two sets of guns' crews.

The light woodwork, ladders, and bulkheads were all destroyed. It was claimed that many valuable documents were captured. Among the papers found were complete working drawings of the Blanco and Cochrane. The ship's log and steam-log had disappeared; it is claimed that they were burned in the furnaces with many other documents. The total duration of the action was 90 minutes. During this time the Huascar lost or had disabled her commander and 3 next senior officers, besides 28 officers and men killed and 48 wounded out of a crew of about 200. She had her steering-gear disabled three distinct times by the enemy's fire, was set on fire in eight different places, had her turret jammed, her right turret gun disabled, and her light guns and Gatling unmanned. A more curious and demoralizing shot-effect can hardly be imagined. Nearly every time that she was struck the greatest possible temporary damage was inflicted, and yet no permanent injury was caused. The armor in this case was only a great disadvantage to her. It served to explode the enemy's projectiles, which it in no case stopped when they struck at any but the smallest angles. The backing and inner skin only served to increase the number of fragments which were driven into the interior of the vessel with deadly effect. On the contrary, the shell that passed through the light iron sides of the forecastle did not explode and did but little damage. The explosion of each shell—and each shell which pierced the armor exploded—set the ship on fire in a new place. This would suggest the great necessity of permanent water-mains with short hose connections in all parts of a vessel. The Chilian small-arm and Nordenfelt gun fire drove every one from the decks and away from the unprotected quarter-deck guns, showing what an important factor that class of fire is to play in all future naval actions. The Chilians had twelve of their best marksmen stationed in each of their fore and main tops. This fire would have been much more terrible had repeating-rifles been used. The fact that good marksmen with rifles drove the crew away from a machine-gun should not be lost sight of. The Nordenfelt, also adopted in the English service, is similar in effects to the Hotchkiss revolving-cannon. It has proved itself not only effective against the *personnel* but also against the *matériel*. This class of arm is certainly of great importance. The mere fact of even the smaller calibers being able to penetrate the sides of any of our unarmored vessels up to eight hundred meters (seventy projectiles a minute), ought to call our attention to it very seriously. The difficulty of ramming when both vessels are under way, even when one is almost unmanageable, is a feature worthy of notice.

It has been asked, of what use would the Whitehead system of torpedoes have been in such an action? The answer would seem to be that the Whitehead or any of the diverging systems would have proved to be dangerous and suicidal. The spar type alone might have been used. The great necessity of having several different means of steering seems also to be well proved, especially some of the systems proposed for steering along the keel, or perhaps even a second rudder, as fitted to the new C class of English corvettes. The places where each of these systems are worked should be in direct telegraphic or voice-tube connection with the position or positions selected for the commanding officer. The position of the commanding officer in action seems another matter worthy of consideration. Near the base of the smoke-stack, the best vertical target on a vessel, seems to be the worst place. The Huascar's tower had another disadvantage; it was between the smoke-stack and the turret, the next best target. In this way it stood an excellent chance of being hit by the projectiles which missed either of these prominent objects. The top of the turret was found to be the best position with us, but a second should certainly be provided. A splinter-grating over the engines would also seem to be suggested by the mass of *débris* which fell on them, but, almost miraculously, did not stop them. It is worthy of note that, while the Chilian vessels could always bring some of their guns to bear on the Huascar, the Huascar found herself in many positions where only sheering would bring her guns to bear on them. In fact, this action tends to prove that an all-round fire, even inferior in single guns, will have a great advantage over a preponderance of fire within only given limits.

The Huascar's voyage south was one continued ovation, and her reception at Valparaiso was accompanied by extensive religious, civic, and military ceremonies. The remains of Admiral Grau were interred at Santiago with full military honors, and throughout South America solemn masses were celebrated for the repose of his soul. The deepest regret at his death was expressed in Peru, Bolivia, and Chile by all classes of people. His record was a bright one. His conduct had endeared him alike to friends, foes, and neutrals. As an example of his disinterested patriotism, he donated all the prize-money which was due him from his several captures to the fund for carrying on the war. He told a friend before leaving Arica for the south on his last expedition that the Huascar would be his tomb, as she proved to be. Admiral Grau, in any service, would have been an honor to the name of gentleman and an ornament to the naval profession.

Commodore Riveros was promoted to the rank of rear-admiral; Commander Latorre to that of captain; and Lieutenant-Commander Castillo to that of commander and placed in command of the Blanco.

The loss of the Huascar roused the Peruvians to a realization of their position. A popular subscription was the outgrowth of this excitement. Men donated their money, women their jewels. The money raised was to buy an iron-clad in Europe, to be called the Admiral Grau.

On the Peruvian side the mastery of the sea pointed out the opportunity of bringing the army, which had hitherto been inactive, into the field, although some maintained that, being in possession of the disputed territory, and having put it out of the power of their enemies to disturb this possession, the objects of the war were accomplished, and it was a good time to propose peace. Re-enforcements of every kind were pushed forward to the army, which now numbered about 16,000 men, well drilled and equipped. Sailing-vessels, to be towed by the steamers, were chartered and taken to Antofagasta. Pack animals were bought in large numbers. The steam transports were supplied with large flat lighters for landing, the larger vessels carrying four secured bottom outwards to their sides, the smaller ones one or two. As an evidence of the effectiveness of this means of landing, the Lautaro regiment, of 1,200 men, with all their matériel, was landed at Coquimbo, and the second battalion of the Coquimbo regiment, numbering 600, embarked in their place on board the transport Itata, in a little less than two hours.

The Blanco was sent to Valparaiso for some slight repairs. About this time the Chilians added to their fleet a rapid steel propeller, brought to Valparaiso loaded with arms, and transformed into the cruiser Angamos. Mounted on this vessel was one of Armstrong's new 8-inch breech-loading rifles.

The allied army at Arica and the south numbered now about 20,000 men.

VII.

FROM THE LANDING AT PISAGUA NOVEMBER 2, 1879, TO THE LANDING AT PACOCHA FEBRUARY 24, 1880.

An expedition, consisting of the men-of-war and ten or twelve transports of all sizes and descriptions, under Commodore Riveros, carrying an army of about seven thousand men, under General Escala, started north from Antofagasta, and appeared off Pisagua on the morning of November 2.

The plan was to make a feint at the seaport of Pisagua, which is situated at the foot of an almost perpendicular bluff twelve hundred feet high. This bluff could be ascended only by the roadway of the railroad or by two narrow zigzag paths; this road and these paths were lined with rifle-pits, the angles being covered by redoubts. Colonel Granier was stationed with twelve hundred Bolivians at the Hospicio, on the summit. The town and landing were defended by two 100-pound R. M. L. gun batteries, situated to the north and south, and several lines of rifle-pits covering the beach. A force of three hundred men occupied the town, where General Buendia himself happened to be at the time of the attack. The main attack was to have been made by a large force, which was to land at Junin, some miles down the coast. Junin was undefended. After landing, this force was to flank the bluffs and attack the enemy in the rear during the night; such a movement being quite possible owing to the almost total disregard of scouting and picketing in South American warfare.

After some delay, seven hundred men were embarked in boats and pulled in towards the landing at the north of the town of Pisagua, the war-ships opening on the batteries and rifle-pits. This force was driven back. Soon afterwards a second force of similar size was sent in, and succeeded in making a landing at the south end of the line. Then followed a feat of arms highly creditable to the pluck and enterprise of the Chilian navy, if not to its discretion. As soon as the soldiers had gained a footing the boats' crews, with their officers, joined them, leaving their boats in imminent danger of destruction from the rocks and surf, to say nothing of the fact that the boats could not return to the ship for re-enforcements.

In a few moments the town, with its defenses, was carried. This was all that was intended, but it was not all that the men intended to do. Step by step, fighting every inch of their way, the whole force pushed up to the bluff in splendid style. The ships joined in and shelled the works ahead of the troops. The result was that in about two hours the heights had been carried, and the allies retreated precipitately up the railroad, leaving behind a large amount of stores of all kinds that had been landed for the army. So unexpected was the victory that even the engines, rolling-stock, and rails of the road were left uninjured. The Chilians immediately landed their main body, and sent some of their transports back for re-enforcements. The large flat scows, lashed to the sides of the transports, greatly expedited this landing. When the force landed at Junin came up they found the Hospicio already in possession of their friends, but the bulk of the enemy had escaped. The Chilians are said to have lost over half the number of the attacking party in storming the heights.

The allies fell back to La Noria and Peña Grande, the terminus of the Iquiqui Railroad, where they were joined by most of the troops from Iquiqui and from the cantonments at Molle and other places within a few days' march, Iquiqui being left to the care of a battalion of national guards. The Chilians moved their advance guard to Agua Santa, near the head of the Pisagua Railroad. The greater part of the main body was moved to the heights of San Francisco, where intrenchments were thrown up to wait for the arrival of re-enforcements. General Escala established his headquarters at Jas Pampas.

Having heard of the capture of Pisagua, President Prado ordered General Daza, with three thousand Bolivians, to move by land and form a junction with General Buendia. This force left Arica and marched as far as the gorge of Camarones, where it turned back, and returned to Arica in a demoralized condition.

General Buendia, finding that his army, which numbered about ten thousand men, was short of provisions, and having been advised of General Daza's advance and probable arrival at about this time near the scene of action, advanced across the thirty miles of desert that separated him from the enemy. The army was organized in three divisions, under Colonels Davila, Bustamente, and Vilegran, the last named commanding the Bolivians. Colonel Davila commanded the advance, which consisted of two of the best regiments of Peruvian regulars.

The Chilian advance-guard at Agua Santa, on the morning of November 19, fell back on the approach of the enemy, who advanced until close to the foot of the heights of San Francisco, where, exhausted and suffering severely from thirst, they were halted and bivouacked. Whilst waiting for water General Buendia went to the advance-guard, and moved them up to reconnoiter the enemy's position; by some mistake a charge was made, and although the troops behaved splendidly they could not stand the Chilian's gun, Gatling and small-arm fire from behind their intrenched position. The advance being unsupported was quickly repulsed. The main body, surprised by the sudden attack and being without a leader, became completely demoralized. It is asserted that the Bolivians were so confused that they opened fire on their retreating allies mistaking them for Chilians. This caused much ill feeling at the time, but when we consider the condition of affairs and the fact that the uniforms of both armies were very similar in color, the mistake seems possible. A general rout now took place, which was not taken advantage of by the Chilians. The loss on the allied side was stated as high as four thousand; but, as nearly the whole Bolivian division started immediately for Bolivia, it was impossible to obtain a correct statement. It is more than probable, however, that the allies lost that number of effectives. During the night Colonel Suarez collected the remnants of the Peruvian army and fell back to the town of Tarapaca.

Iquiqui was evacuated, and a regiment of Chilians with the iron-clad Cochrane sent to occupy it on the 22d.

On the 18th of November the Blanco captured the gunboat Pilcomayo in a greatly damaged condition, Commander Ferreyras having made all manner of attempts to destroy her.

The O'Higgins and Magellanes appeared off Mollendo, where they cut the submarine cable, thus severing communication between Arica and Lima.

On the 29th of November, President Prado suddenly returned to Lima, having turned over his command to Admiral Montero.

The day after the battle of San Francisco the Chilians sent a force of about two thousand men to reconnoiter the enemy. Disregarding his orders, the commander of this force pushed up to the heights above the town of Tarapaca, where his men arrived in an exhausted condition and without water. Tarapaca is situated in a valley surrounded by high hills. The Peruvians had evacuated, and were already moving north when they were informed of the condition of the Chilians, who had entered the town, parked their guns, and bivouacked without a picket line. They returned and fell suddenly upon the Chilians, routing them completely and capturing a light battery of Krupp guns which were not even out of park.

Having gained this success and being entirely out of ammunition, the Peruvians again started on their march to Arica, where about three thousand of them arrived, unmolested on the way, ragged, hungry, and most of them without arms. General Buendia and Colonel Suarez, his chief of staff, were immediately placed under arrest.

General Campero with his division of Bolivians, who had been supposed to be near the line of the Loa, reappeared in La Paz about this time.

The Chilians now had complete possession of the rich province of Tarapaca.

Leaving a small force in garrison in the town of Tarapaca, the main body of the army was withdrawn to Pisagua and Iquiqui, to which places the inhabitants and shipping began also to return. The army was re-enforced from the south until it numbered about seventeen thousand men. The smallpox, that had been raging on the coast for months, and the hot summer weather caused a considerable loss to the army of occupation.

The men-of-war were moved up the coast, and Arica, Islay, and Ilo were blockaded, Mollendo being kept under surveillance.

This blockade cut Arica off from communication with the north except by mule-paths from Arequipa. General Daza had about three thousand men at Tacna, and Admiral Montero about four thousand at Arica.

On the 17th of December the Union left Callao loaded with ammunition and stores for the army at Arica, her commander's orders being to get as near that place as possible and land his cargo. This he succeeded in doing at Ilo, from which place they were taken by rail to Moquegua, and thence on muleback to Arica.

President Prado suddenly left Callao on the evening of December 19, for parts unknown, since ascertained to be the United States. All sorts of rumors were rife in regard to this departure.

Señor La Puerta, who was in poor health, succeeded to the supreme authority. General La Cotera, minister of war, a man of great personal courage, became the prime mover of the Government.

During the afternoon of December 21 a revolution, which had been smouldering in Peru for years, broke out, Señor Don Nicholas Pierola, a doctor of laws and an ex-minister of state, who was at this time colonel of one of the new regiments, being its leader. The Government party, headed by General La Cotera, soon found itself shut up in the palace with a few troops. Colonel Pierola at the head of his own regiment and that of his friend, Colonel Agueras, after attacking the Government troops in Lima, moved down to Callao during the night and took possession of that place in the morning, meeting the slightest possible resistance. The same day the Government capitulated, and Pierola declared himself supreme chief of the Republic with dictatorial powers.

Following the revolution in Peru came one in Bolivia, which placed General Campero in power. Shortly afterwards, during General Daza's absence from Tacna, he having been summoned to Arica by Admiral Montero, the troops were marched out to bathe, leaving their arms in their barracks. Colonel Camacho, who was in temporary command, then with his own regiment seized all the barracks and declared himself commander-in-chief. General Daza soon afterwards left Arica alone, and became a refugee in Peru.

About this time the Blanco, Amazonas, and some of the smaller vessels began to operate to the northward of Callao, visiting the guano deposits at the Lobos Islands where they stopped the loading, as they also did at Independencia Bay. The Amazonas succeeded in capturing a large torpedo-boat, which had been sent across the isthmus to Panama, where it was put together and allowed to proceed to sea. These raids kept Callao and Lima in a continued state of disquietude. The Government displayed some activity in collecting raw levies about the capital. The Union, Atahualpa, and transports were moved into shoal water and behind the mole, in order to be in positions of safety. Had the place been strongly blockaded, these vessels could not have been more effectually kept in port.

On the 6th of January a force of about five hundred Chilians was landed at Ilo for the purpose of capturing the stores brought by the Union, which were supposed to be there still, and of destroying the railroad and rolling-stock. The whole command embarked in a train and went up the line to Moquegua, returning the next day; they re-embarked without having accomplished anything.

On the 7th of January a serious landslide on the Oroya Railroad stopped the running of the trains, effectually closing communication between Lima and the interior.

VIII.

FROM THE LANDING AT PACOCHA TO THE CAPTURE OF ARICA, JUNE 6, 1880.

The Chilians embarked 12,000 men in 20 transports at Pisagua, and started north on the 24th of February, 1880. The next day they landed 9,000 infantry and 600 cavalry at Pacocha, a small town about 60 miles north of Arica, the seaport of Moquegua, with which place it is connected by a railroad. At the same time 3,000 men were landed at Vitor, situated about 20 miles south of Pacocha. As soon as the men were landed the transports were sent south for provisions and stores, with which to attempt the severe march across a desert country. This was no small undertaking, where even water had to be provided. On the 12th of March the advance-guard, under General Baquedano, consisting of four regiments of infantry, two squadrons of cavalry, and eighteen pieces of artillery, started inland towards Moquegua, and after a painful march across the desert of the Hospicio, camped at Alto-del-Conde at 8 a. m., March 15, where they remained until the 19th, to recuperate. In the mean time the surrounding country was thoroughly reconnoitered. On the 19th an advance was made to Catalina, situated about nine miles from Moquegua. At 8.30 the next morning another move was made, and in three hours Moquegua was occupied without resistance. From the heights of Alto de la Villa, which command the old town of Moquegua, and which is fast becoming the actual site of the city since the earthquake of 1868, the Peruvian forces could be seen occupying the strong position of Los Angeles, so noted in South American warfare.

Los Angeles is situated on one of the spurs of Mount Torata. There Colonel Gamarro, having abandoned the less tenable position of Moquegua, had intrenched his force of 2,000 men. This position was most important, as it covered the line of retreat of Montero and the army of Arica and Tacna on Puno and Arequipa, and left communication open for General Beingolea's army, which had reached Ica on its march to the relief of Arica. The Peruvian position was in a triangle formed by the river Ilo and its branches. The front, of about four miles, was accessible only up a steep incline of over one thousand feet; the left was protected by a deep ravine, and the right was covered by a range of almost impassable mountains. A front attack was rendered still more difficult from the fact that the ascent had to be first approached down a sandy slope completely exposed to the Peruvian fire, and even then a ravine had to be crossed. The Peruvians had dug seven lines of rifle-pits across their front, in which the Grau regiment was deployed. Two companies were posted to cover the Samequa ravine on the left. The remainder of the force was held in reserve. The right was undefended except by the mountains. On the 21st the Chilian army was moved to within rifle-range. At 9 p. m. Colonel Muñoz, with seven companies of the Second Regulars, one battalion of the Santiago regiment, Fuentes's battery of Krupp mountain-guns, and 300 cavalry, started round by way of Tumilca to turn the Peruvian left. By some mistake the road was missed, and at daylight the Peruvians discovered their enemies in the Samequa ravine. Fuentes's battery was immediately posted on the opposite side of the ravine. Colonel Muñoz, with the Santiago battalion and one company of regulars, attacked the Peruvians, whilst Lieutenant-Colonel Del Cuato held the remainder in reserve. In the mean time the Atacama regiment, composed almost entirely of mountaineers and miners, had forced its way, by almost superhuman efforts, up the mountains on the Peruvian right, arriving at the crest at 6 a. m. At this time two batteries of artillery, under Lieutenant-Colonel Novoa, opened on the Peruvian front, and General Baquedano attacked the rifle-pits with the Bulnes regiment and second battalion of the Santiago deployed. The Grau regiment of Peruvians, finding itself enfiladed by the Atacama regiment, retreated before the front attacks of General Baquedano; at the same time Muñoz headed a gallant and successful bayonet charge on the Peruvian left. Finding itself worsted on all sides, the Peruvian army fell back in disorder on Ilubaya, the Chilians ocupying Yacango, and the next day Torata.

Whilst these events were transpiring about Moquegua the Chilians were pushing the war elsewhere. In order to keep Admiral Montero's attention engaged, and to prevent his sending any of his force to re-enforce Colonel Gamarro, an attack was made on Arica, on the 27th of February, by the Huascar and Magellanes. The Huascar ran in towards the Moro, engaging the batteries on that bluff and the monitor Manco Capac anchored off the town. Early in the engagement the Huascar received a shot in her hull. Observing that troops were actually leaving in the railway trains, the Chilian fire was directed upon them, causing their return to the town. The fight now became very warm, seven men being killed and nine wounded on board the Huascar. Not desiring to expose their vessels any longer to the heavy plunging fire of the shore batteries, the Chilians withdrew, but were followed by the Manco Capac. Seeing this, the Huascar was again headed in shore, and engaged her antagonist at two hundred yards range. The Huascar attempted to ram, but desisted from the attempt on noticing that her opponent was accompanied by a torpedo-boat; she thereupon drew off and steamed around in a circle. In doing this a shot struck the new foremast which had been put in her at Valparaiso, to replace the tripod removed by Admiral Grau, so that she was again reduced to one mast, and came near having her turret disabled. Another shot killed her commander, Captain Manuel Thompson, a valuable officer, of English descent, who had distinguished himself in the capture of the Covadonga from the Spanish, and who had returned to the service of his country, from civil life, at the outbreak of this war. After Thompson's death Lieutenant Valverde assumed command, and after continuing the combat, without important results, for about an hour, withdrew. Captain Condell, of Covadonga fame, was now transferred from the command of the Magellanes to that of the Huascar.

On the 17th of March the Peruvian corvette Union, under Captain Villavicencio, gallantly ran the blockade at Arica, and succeeded in landing a valuable cargo of supplies, although constantly exposed to the fire of the blockaders for seven hours, the time required for unloading and coaling. At one time the fire became so severe that the authorities on shore advised the captain to run his vessel aground. One shot struck the deck, breaking three beams, damaging the smoke-stack and endangering the boilers. The Chilians expected the Union to run out to the northward, and made their preparations accordingly. Villavicencio, on the contrary, started for the southward at full speed, in broad daylight, at 5 p. m., and succeeded in reaching Callao in safety. This shows what pluck and speed combined will do.

About this time the Chilians paid another visit to the Chincha Islands, where, in spite of the danger of capture, some adventurous merchantmen had been loading guano. They destroyed the chutes and launches.

On the 12th of March Colonel Silva, the Bolivian commander at Viacha, revolted with his troops against the Government of Campero. The revolution was suppressed, not without, however, greatly retarding the march of four battalions intended for the re-enforcement of Gamarro at Moquegua. Colonel Camacho, the Bolivian commander-in-chief, accused Silva in a very strong letter of having caused a duplication of the Camarones affair, and of having been the cause of the perilous position in which the allied cause was placed by the entire cutting off of Montero's army of the south.

On the 8th of April, all the preparations were completed for the advance on Tacna, and the country thoroughly reconnoitered by the cavalry. In executing this service Colonel Dublé Almieda, chief of staff, with twenty-five cavalrymen, were surprised at Locumba by foragers under Colonel Albaracin-Duble, only four men being able to cut their way out. The first Chilian division, under Colonel Amengual, started south by the coast roads towards Sitana, whilst the cavalry of the second division moved from Moquegua towards Siuta and Sagayo, in order to turn Locumba. On the 11th the first and second divisions occupied Locumba, and the third division moved out of Pacocha. Colonel Vergara, of the National Guards, engaged the cavalry under Albaracin at Sama on the 18th, completely routing him, with a loss of 100 men and a large number of cattle that were intended for the garrison of Tacna. The Chilian cavalry was then pushed on without opposition close up to Tacna. The fourth division moved out of Pacocha on the 18th.

We will now leave the Chilians moving on Tacna, in order to follow the course of events on the sea. Encouraged by the success of the Union, the Oroya (armed rapid transport) was sent south from Callao with a valuable cargo of munitions of war, including 7,000 rifles and 20 field-guns (Krupp and Armstrong). These were safely landed at Islay, and were used to equip General Biengolea's army, which now numbered about 7,000 men, and was located about Arequipa. The Oroya then went to Tocopilla, where she captured the little steamer Duende, belonging to the Nitrate Company; she then went north, reaching Callao April 9.

The same day a Chilian squadron, under Rear-Admiral Riveros, consisting of the Blanco (flag-ship), Huascar, Angamos, Pilcomayo, Matthias Cousiño, and torpedo-boats Guacolda and Janequeo, was moving down the coast towards Callao. At 3 p. m. the torpedo-boats, convoyed by the Huascar, were pushed ahead. The Guacolda, Lieutenant Commanding Goni, broke down and became separated from her convoy, but meeting the fleet at about 8 p. m. was repaired and again pushed ahead alone, arriving off San Lorenzo Island at 1 a. m. After waiting for the Janequeo (which it was afterwards learned had missed the port by about ten miles to the northward) for about an hour, Goni determined to run in toward the vessels. Approaching the usual man-of-war anchorage from the southward, he made out the neutral-men-of-war. Shortly afterwards, in the dark, he ran into and sank a fishing-boat, from which he saved three men, who were forced to point out the position of the Union, which, with the Atahualpa, Chalaco, and Oroya, were at anchor outside of the Muelle d'Arsena, or stone docks. Captain Villavicencio had moored the Union and surrounded her with a strong torpedo-boom. Unfortunately for Goni, in the collision with the fishing-boat one of his bow spars was carried away, so that when he struck the Union's boom protection and exploded his torpedo he became powerless to injure the vessel itself, although he completely opened a passage to her, which he could have used himself, or which could have been used by a companion, if he had had one. The vessels immediately opened a heavy small-arm and machine-gun fire on the torpedo-boat, which was forced to withdraw.

The next day the Rimac, Chalaco, Oroya, Union, and Atahualpa were moored behind the breakwater of the stone docks, where the Talisman, Apurimac (an old wooden frigate), Marañon (school-hulk), and several smaller vessels had already been placed.

At 6 a. m., April 10, the Chilian fleet appeared off Callao, and Admiral Riveros sent, by flag of truce, a notice to the senior Peruvian officer that he had come to blockade the port of Callao and the bays in the vicinity, that eight days would be allowed for the withdrawal of neutral merchant vessels, and that, as in the course of events it might become necessary for him to bombard the city, he gave timely warning for the removal of non-combatants. Similar notices were sent to the dean of the consular corps and to the senior foreign naval officer. The foreign diplomatic authorities asked an extension of the time allowed to neutral vessels to fifteen days, and special warning in case of intention to bombard. Admiral Riveros answered that he would extend the time to ten days, and that he considered his first notice as all that was necessary for the removal of non-combatants. He promised, however, that he would not initiate hostilities until after the 20th, the day on which the port was to be cleared.

The defenses of Callao at this time—not including the guns of the men-of-war, which were almost completely masked behind the stone pier—consisted of a series of batteries of almost every system and period, extending in the form of a crescent around the shores of the bay for about three miles, the town being at the middle point. The most southerly one, situated on the end of the point and commanding the best range of the usual Chilian position, was called the Dos de Mayo; it had but lately been finished, and consisted of an immense pit in the rubble and gravel, the inside faces being revetted with sand bags. The gun platforms were on heavy crib-work resting on piles, the platforms themselves being of stone. In this work there were two 20-inch smoothbore muzzle-loading Rodmans—one of the navy, the other of the army pattern—mounted on our ordinary iron carriages, to which additional compressors were fitted. Extreme charges were used in these guns, but the powder was of inferior quality. These guns commanded about seven-eighths of the horizon, including the bays of Callao and Chorillos, and the Boqueron Passage connecting them. The next two batteries were similar in construction, one facing on Callao Bay, the other on that of Chorillos. They were named Pierola and Tarapaca, and were each mounted with two heavy 15-inch smooth-bore muzzle-loading Dahlgrens. Next came the Torre del Merced, a monitor turret, mounted on masonry, and containing two 10-inch muzzle-loading Armstrong rifles. Next an old-fashioned brick fort, called Santa Rosa, in which were mounted two 11-inch muzzle-loading Blakely rifles. This was flanked by batteries armed with old-fashioned 32-pounders, some of which were the highly-ornamented bronze guns brought over by the Spaniards. Next in the town was the castle, the only important part of which for modern warfare was two masonry towers or turrets, each armed with two 11-inch muzzle-loading Blakely rifles. Guns protected by sand-bags were mounted on the sea-pier of the docks or mole; these were five 15-inch smooth-bore muzzle-loading Dahlgrens, two 11-inch smooth-bore muzzle-loading Dahlgrens, and two 32-pounders. Next on the right of the town was the Ayacucho fort—similar to the Santa Rosa—armed with one 11-inch muzzle-loading Blakely rifle and one 15-inch smooth-bore muzzle-loading Dahlgren. Next a monitor turret, called Junin, mounted with two 10-inch Armstrong muzzle-loading rifles, and on the extreme right a new sand-bag battery, called the Rimac, mounted with four 15-inch smooth-bore muzzle-loading Dahlgrens.

Callao was deserted by almost all of its non-combatant inhabitants, most of the shops were closed, and all business was transacted in Lima. Ambulances were established and the volunteer fire department kept constantly on duty. An order was issued forbidding boating after sundown. All communication with Lima from the sea being cut off, the authorities, fearing a great rise in the price of provisions, issued a decree on the 14th of April fixing their prices.

April 20, at noon, the ten days' grace expired, the last merchant ship had left, and the foreign men-of-war had moved at 11 a. m. to a position off the river Rimac, out of the line of fire. To this place a number of hulks were also taken, which had been provisioned and fitted up to receive refugees in case of an attack on Lima.

At 1.30 p. m., April 22, the Chilian squadron got under way from its moorings near San Lorenzo Island, and stood over towards the batteries. The Pilcomayo took position north of the center of the bay, next to the southward the Angamos, next the Huascar; the two first vessels being armed with the new Armstrong breech-loading rifles. The Blanco was held in reserve, covering the line. At 2.05 p. m. the Huascar opened fire, followed by the Pilcomayo and Angamos. The objective point was the vessels behind the mole; the range between five and seven thousand yards. The firing was accurate, and but few shells failed to explode. The Peruvians returned the fire from seventeen heavy guns on shore and from the pivot-guns of the Union, but all of these projectiles fell short. The firing continued until 4.50 p. m., when the flag-ship signaled to retire from action. The Chilians fired one hundred and seventy shots, the Peruvians one hundred and twenty-seven, of which seventy-eight were fired by the "Union's" Armstrong muzzle-loading rifles. The Marañon had a shell exploded in her hold, The Rimac, Chalaco, Talisman, and Union were struck several times. and several shells passing over exploded in the Oroya Railroad station, and in the town beyond. Admiral Riveros did not seem much inclined to risk his vessels, and probably intended the action more to show the Peruvians what his new long range guns could do than as a serious attempt to destroy vessels which he hoped eventually to capture.

Many reports in regard to torpedoes had been circulated, and the Chilians were continually on the watch for them. Permanent moorings with buoys were laid down off the end of the island, to which the blockaders rode during the day-time, getting under way every night, leaving two small vessels to guard the moorings. Two torpedo-boats were kept on patrol in the bay at night, and during foggy weather these often ran in close to the mole and among the foreign men-of-war. The Peruvians probably did lay down a few torpedoes, but they were placed close to the shore. . They certainly made preparations for torpedoing, and were moderately successful in the use of that weapon. They were provided with several regular torpedo-boats and had a number of launches and small tugs fitted up for torpedo work. These were sometimes used for patrol duty. They were also provided with torpedoes of the Lay system. Two serious accidents occurred to their torpedo corps. One of the Herreshoff boats was run into the mole and sunk, and on the 1st of May a serious explosion took place at the torpedo manufactory at Ancon.

At seven o'clock on the morning of May 5 the Amazonas, being under way in the bay on guard duty, discovered two small buoys covered by shields. These floated about eighteen inches out of the water at a little distance from each other. The commanding officer of the Amazonas sent a boat to inspect them, and the admiral sent in the torpedo-boat Guacolda, which opened on them with her machine-gun, exploding one of the buoys with great violence. The other was towed ashore and, on grounding, exploded. These torpedoes were probably intended to foul the bows of vessels.

At 1.25 p. m., May 10, the Blanco, Huascar, Pilcomayo, Amazonas, and Angamos got under way and steamed over towards the batteries. The corvette O'Higgins took up a position in the Boqueron Passage to shell the 20-inch Dos de Mayo battery—range, 4,500 yards; the Blanco took position 4,000 yards from the same battery with the same object. The Huascar took position at the head of the line to the northward of the center of the bay, with the Pilcomayo, Amazonas, and Angamos between her and the Blanco. The objective point of these vessels were the ships behind the mole—range, about 5,500 yards. The Huascar afterwards filled her double bottom with water, reducing her free-board to 2 feet, and changed her range to 3,000 yards. Whilst at this close range she was pierced by a shot as she rolled, and was only prevented from sinking by her water-tight bulkheads. Admiral Riveros feared the effect of the 20-inch shot on the Huascar, and therefore placed her farthest from the Dos de Mayo battery. The action continued until 4.45 p. m., up to which time the Chilians fired 400 shots and the Peruvians 200. With the exception of the shot already mentioned, two more that glanced off of the same vessel, and one that cut her main rigging, the Chilians came out of the action without injury. The Peruvians were almost as fortunate. The Union was set on fire by a shell, but the fire was soon extinguished. The Saucy Jack, a small prize bark, was sunk. A boat going to rescue her crew was struck, two of her people being killed and four wounded. A few shells exploded in the town. Seventy per cent. of the Chilian projectiles struck within the mole or passed over it. About 20 Peruvians were killed. The O'Higgins managed with her broadside battery to drive the men away from the 20-inch guns several times.

At 2.30 a. m., May 25, a Peruvian old-type steam-launch, that formerly belonged to the ill-fated Independencia, commanded by Lieutenant Galvez, with a crew of sixteen men, and armed with a Gardner gun in the bow and a 2-inch breech-loading rifle in the stern, came suddenly upon the Chilian steel Thornycroft torpedo-launch Guacolda, which had a speed of 11 knots and was fitted with three spar-torpedoes, one right ahead and one on each bow. The Peruvian started at full speed for the mole as soon as he made out his enemy. The Janequeo, a steel Yarrow torpedo-launch, with a speed of 18 knots, now appeared on the scene, and passing ahead of her sister boat exploded her bow torpedo under the Peruvian's counter; at the same moment Lieutenant Galvez and Surgeon Ugarte exploded a torpedo on the Janequeo's bow, which opened a large leak and killed two men. Her commander, Lieutenant Senoret, managed to get her alongside of a lighter, where she sank. Lieutenant Goni, in the Guacolda, continued to chase the Independencia, which kept up a heavy fire from her small-arms and stern gun. At last the Peruvians, finding their launch sinking, ceased firing and surrendered. Goni sent his dingey to her rescue and succeeded in saving Lieutenant Galvez, seriously wounded, and seven of the crew. It was not till this time that Goni missed his consort; but thinking that she had returned to the fleet, he went back to the flag-ship, put the wounded and prisoners on board, and finding that the Janequeo had not returned went in search of her. As he approached the floating-dock he met Lieutenant Senoret and his crew coming out in two small boats which they had picked up alongside of the hulk Callao.

On the morning of May 27, whilst a Peruvian flag-of-truce boat was carrying on shore Lieutenant Galvez, who had been released on account of his severe wounds, two Peruvian launches attempted to grapple and raise the Janequeo. Seeing this, the Huascar steamed in and was fired upon by the shore batteries. The Huascar headed towards the mole, and the Peruvians at work on the sunken launch fled. At 10.42 the Huascar opened fire, and at 11.02 the Angamos opened at a range of four miles. The Chilian fire did some damage, setting fire to a house and killing several persons. The Huascar fired at ranges of from two and three-quarters to three miles; the Angamos, with her 8-inch breech-loading Armstrong rifle, from three and a half to four and a half. Later in the day the Peruvians again attempted to raise the launch, but were driven off by the Angamos, which approached quite near to them under cover of the foreign men-of-war.

On the morning of May 30 the torpedo-launch Guacolda went in and drove off the Peruvian launches that were at work on her sunken consort. She then remained over the spot, and a diver went down, who placed a torpedo, by which the bone of contention was destroyed. Whilst this was going on the Peruvian boats were re-enforced by two other launches, and then by a small tug; all of these were armed with a 2 or 3 inch breech-loading rifle and machine guns. This flotilla approached the Chilian launch to within pistol-shot, when they fired a gun. The Chilian boat withdrew at full speed. At this time, about 6.42 a. m., the Pilcomayo opened on the vessels behind the mole. She was soon joined by the Huascar and Angamos. All of the shore batteries opened fire. The Angamos did some splendid firing. The Chilians kept their vessels at long range; the Huascar, from seven thousand and ninety-five yards to six thousand four hundred and eighty-six; the Pilcomayo, from six thousand two hundred and eighty-four yards to six thousand eight hundred; the Angamos being seven thousand and ninety-five yards from the nearest 20-inch battery. The Peruvians, seeing that their enemy was determined to engage outside of their range, towed the Athaualpa out about half a mile, but her shot still fell short about one mile. The Chilians succeeded in sinking the school-ship Tumbez and a hulk with 700 tons of Government coal, both of these vessels being behind the mole.

The blockade of the coast was maintained by the O'Higgins cruising between Ancon and Chancay; the ships off Callao; the Chacabuco and Covadonga off the coast of the province of Arequipa, and the Cochrane and Magellanes off Arica.

It is time to leave the blockading fleet and see what is doing in the south. We left the four divisions of the Chilian army moving on Tacna. As soon as the main body reached Sama the base of supplies was moved to Ite, a small harbor about 24 miles from that place and connected with it by good roads, additional re-enforcements were brought from Pisagua, and the wounded and sick were sent south.

General Campero, the President of Bolivia, having put down the revolt at Viacha, had succeeded in joining Admiral Montero with between 2,000 and 3,000 men. There was, besides, a chance of succor from General Benigolea, last heard from near Arequipa, where his men had been thoroughly equipped from the cargo of the Oroya. The allied army at Tacna, numbering about fourteen thousand of all arms, was commanded by General Campero. Admiral Montero commanded the right, composed of Peruvians, and General Camacho the left, composed of Bolivians. The Chilian army, of about equal numbers, was commanded by General Biquedano. The allies were posted along the crest and advanced slope of a line of hills northwest of Tacna and parallel to the valley of the same name. These hills were connected with an immense sandy plain, over which the Chilians were advancing, by a gradual slope which had been strongly fortified. The southern extremity of the line of hills occupied by the left of the allies terminated with a steep slope, that was considered inaccessible. The right bent back towards the city, and was trongly intrenched and defended by artillery. The advanced line of works consisted of rifle pits. About 1,050 yards in rear was a strong line of trenches, extending along the whole front about 4½ miles. On the right, this line was thrown slightly to the front in order to connect with a well-constructed fort placed on a slight eminence, almost unassailable in front on account of the heavy sand, but easily approached from the rear. This fort enfiladed the whole line. Covering this fort and so placed as to take the first line of intrenchments in reverse, was a well-constructed sand-bag redoubt. On the crest of the hills was a second line of intrenchments, broken and echeloned to the right and rear. The artillery was distributed along the line, some of the lighter batteries covering the line of rifle-pits. The Bolivian cavalry, for some unaccountable reason, was posted on the extreme end of the line of hills to the left, where it could not possibly be brought into action as cavalry. The Peruvian cavalry covered the right of the line.

At 9.50 a. m., May 26, the Chilian artillery, having taken its position at between 3,500 and 4,000 yards from the Peruvian line, opened fire. The First and Second Divisions, then about 4 miles off, were ordered to advance against the allies' line. This they did in double column of companies, the First Division being covered by the Valparaiso battalion deployed as skirmishers; the Second by one company from each of its battalions. At 11.10 the First Division was within rifle-range, and deployed in line of battle in the following order of regiments: Navales on the extreme right, Valparaiso; Esmeralda, and Chilian in reserve. Shortly afterwards the Second Division deployed, the Second Regulars connecting with the Esmeralda, then the Santiago, and on the extreme left the Atacama. At 11.21 the line reached the base of the slope, the right being only about 400 yards from the Bolivian left, and the Atacama regiment 1,000 yards from the Peruvian right. It was not until now that the allies opened fire, a great mistake in modern warfare, especially as the Chilians advanced in close order. This fact is amply proved by the Atacamas losing one-fourth of their number between 1,000 and 600 yards.

The First Division took up the double and charged the first line of the Bolivians. The Navales regiment, turning its left, opened a heavy enfilading fire, which, coupled with the front attack of the other battalions, caused a retreat, in which the artillery was abandoned. The Second Regulars opened fire at 600 yards, and advanced to 80 yards from the rifle-pits, when Lieutenant-Colonel Del Canto ordered a bayonet charge, and caused the Peruvians in his front to fall back on the trenches. The Santiago and Atacama regiments moved rapidly to the front, but they were opposed by a murderous fire from the guns and machine-guns of the fort, and to a tremendous small-arm fire from the trenches and redoubt, and were soon checked. In the mean time Montero moved up all of his reserves, and opposed his whole force to the 4,000 Chilians who had come into action. The Third and Fourth Divisions, by some error having been retarded in their march, could not re-enforce the fighting line at this important moment. The Esmeralda regiment began to break, as its ammunition was giving out. These men were provided with 100 rounds when they went into the fight instead of the 130 usually issued. This was not a green regiment, and this tremendous expenditure of ammunition in a few minutes points out the great importance of ammunition reserves. Fortunately for the Chilians, the Second Regulars were on the left of the Esmeraldas, and the Valparaiso, a regiment made up of Valparaiso policemen—all old soldiers—was on its right. These sustained the action against heavy odds for about an hour, retreating in perfect order. The Bolivians succeeded in cutting off the right wing of the Navales regiment, which had been thrown around their flank, but the Chilian Grenadier cavalry regiment made a brilliant charge and rescued their comrades. The Navales then reformed in rear of the Valparaiso and soon retook its position in line. The whole of the Atacama regiment had been deployed as skirmishers on the left to meet a flank attack from the Peruvians, it having been found that they could not maintain their position in solid line. Things were looking very badly for the Chilians, when, at 12.30, the Third Division arrived. The marines were sent to support the right, the Chacabuco regiment the center, and the Coquimbo regiment moved up in rear of the Atacama. The Esmeralda regiment was reformed, and again took its position in line. The offensive was resumed by the Chilians. The Fourth Division came up, and being in close column suffered considerably from the Peruvian fire, intended probably for the first line. Fontecilla's battery was moved up on the left, and covered its deployment in the following order from right to left: Zapadores, Riflemen-of-the-Desert, Lautaro. The reserve division, consisting of the First, Third, and Fourth Regulars and the Bulnes battalion, appeared in rear of the center of the line; but it was not necessary to deploy them, as at one o'clock a grand advance was made all along the line, and the riflemen carried the fort. The whole allied line retreated, passing rapidly through Tacna and making for the mountains. The Chilians lost in this action 2,000 men, mostly from the First and Second Divisions; the Atacama and Second

Regular Regiments, which had already been greatly reduced by previous service, losing about half of their effective strength. The Bolivian losses were not given, but it is known that Daza's veteran regiment, the Colorado, was almost annihilated. The Peruvians lost 1,000 men killed and 1,500 wounded, the losses falling heaviest on the Zepita and Carnavaro regiments, which were opposed to the Second Chilian Regulars. Only 400 prisioners were taken. The Peruvian Red Cross ambulances were admirably administered, giving prompt care to their own wounded, and to those of the Chilians left on the ground when they were repulsed.

The Chilian cavalry was pushed down the Arica Railroad immediately after the battle. During the night they reached the Chacayuta River, where the road crosses by a bridge. This bridge had been destroyed by the Peruvians, and the approach to it planted with dynamite mines, one of which was exploded on the approach of the Chilians. Warned by this explosion, which was ineffectual, the operator being deceived by the darkness, an immediate search was made, and the operator discovered in a small hut where the firing-board was placed. Nine torpedoes were then traced and unearthed. The 2d of June, General Baquedano pushed the Reserve Division, consisting of the First, Third, and Fourth Regulars and Bulnes battalion, down the road, which had been repaired as far as the bridge.

The town of Arica is situated on a sandy plain by the sea. Rising out of this plain to the southward of the town is a hill called the Moro. The sea-face and north, and south sides of this hill are almost precipitous, and reach an elevation of about 1,200 feet; the east side is a gradual slope. The plateau at the top of this hill formed the citadel of the defenses; its rim was crowned with sand-bag batteries, in which heavy guns were mounted. Around the three land sides of the hill, including the town, was a line of forts and trenches. The garrison, commanded by Colonel Bolognesi—a Peruvian of Italian descent—consisted of about 2,000 men, besides whom there were a number of wounded and sick in the ambulance hospital in the town. Besides the land defenses, the monitor Manco Capac, commanded by Captain Lagomarsino, was anchored off the north fort.

By the 5th of June Arica was invested on the land side by the Reserve Division, re-enforced by the Lautaro regiment, and from the sea by the squadron, under Captain Latorre, consisting of the Cochrane, Magellanes, Covadonga, and Loa. Colonel Bolognesi was summoned to surrender, but declined to do so.

On the morning of June 6 the Chilian field batteries opened fire at seven thousand yards, but were soon silenced by the heavy artillery of the Peruvians. The ships then opened fire, the Cochrane from the center of the bay, 1,000 yards from the Moro, the Magellanes and Covadonga closing to 2,500 yards, and the Loa firing from 8,000. The shore batteries turned their attention to the ships. The Covadonga was struck twice near the water-line by 150-pounder projectiles and considerably damaged. A shell entered one of the Cochrane's ports and exploded, setting fire to two cartridges; by the explosion of the shell and that of the cartridges 27 men were wounded. After having fired 80 shots, and been fired at 74 times, the Chilian ships were withdrawn until the next day, when an assault was to be made. The plan of attack was as follows: The Lautaro regiment was to attack the northern forts, the first battalion that of San José, the second that of Santa Rosa. The Bulnes battalion was to act as a support to the artillery and a reserve to the Lautaro regiment. The First, Third, and Fourth Regulars were to attack the south forts. The First was to be held in reserve; the first battalion of the Third was to attack the Ciudadela fort, covered by the second battalion, and the Fourth regiment was to attack the other two forts. All were in position at daylight, and the Chilian troops had advanced within 1,200 yards of the Ciudadela fort when they were discovered by the pickets. The action became general. In the assault on the Ciudadela fort a dynamite torpedo was exploded, which killed a number of men, and so exasperated the Chilians that the whole garrison of the fort, 450 in number, are said to have been slaughtered. The Fourth carried its forts, but as the men occupied the easterly one it was blown up. In the mean time the Lautaro regiment had captured Forts San José and Santa Rosa, and the Peruvians, at 7 a. m. only held the east forts and the Moro. One of the east forts which commanded the Moro was next captured by the Fourth Regiment, and the others were abandoned. Colonel Bolognesi, assisted by the unfortunate Captain Moore, of Independencia fame, rallied the garrison and the refugees from the other forts, and made a magnificent defense, which was unsuccessful in the end.

The Manco Capac, which had borne but little part in the defense, was blown up by her commander when he saw the capture of the Moro. The crew gave themselves up on board the transport Itata. A torpedo-boat attempted to escape, but was driven ashore by the Toro and blown up by her crew.

The Peruvians lost 700 men killed, 100 wounded, and 600 prisoners. The Chilians lost 400 men, all told.

Having utterly destroyed the Army of the South, having conquered the whole of the rich Department of Moquegua from Peru, being in possession of the entire Bolivian seaboard, and having blockaded Callao and the principal sea-ports of the north, the main army went into summer quarters.

5 W S A.

IX.

FROM THE FALL OF ARICA TO THE FALL OF LIMA. JANUARY 17, 1881.

On the 3d of July a small coaster, or Huacho packet, as they are called, was seen to leave the port of Callao and to steal along the coast to the northward. The armed transport Loa, which had joined the blockading squadron after the fall of Arica, was sent in chase. Shortly afterwards three men were seen to leave the coaster in a small boat and land through the surf. The small vessel was then taken possession of, and found to be loaded with fruit, vegetables, and poultry—a valuable prize to a blockading force. She was taken alongside of the Loa, and the work of unloading commenced. In a few moments a tremendous explosion took place; the Loa was soon seen to sink by the stern, careening to port, but righting with her mast-heads above water when she reached the bottom. It is supposed that the packet contained a large case of dynamite fitted with friction fuses, from which wires led to some of the packages of the cargo. In unloading, as intended, one of these packages was probably lifted and the torpedo exploded, blowing a large hole in the Loa's side and causing the loss of 145 officers and men out of a crew of 200.

Large amounts of war material of all kinds were being run into the Peruvian ports, some even into Callao.

On the 24th of August the neutral men-of-war commenced to transport refugees from Callao to Chimbote, which became the terminus of the Pacific Steam Navigation Company's line.

August 30 and 31 and September 1 the Angamos engaged the batteries, generally at four-miles range. On the last day the Union's boilers were struck, and the torpedo depot-hulk was sunk. The shore batteries always returned the fire, but their shot fell about a mile short.

September 3 the Blanco, O'Higgins, and Angamos engaged the batteries. Several Peruvian armed tugs came out from behind the mole apparently with the intention of making a torpedo attack, but returned again without accomplishing anything. The largest tug was sunk by a shot from the Angamos as she passed behind the mole.

A division of Chilians about 3,000 strong, under Colonel Patricio Lynch (actually a captain in the navy), landed at Chimbote on the 10th of September. After occupying the railroad station and telegraph office, they proceeded inland to a large sugar plantation called Palo Seco. There they demanded $100,000 in silver as ransom money, threatening, if it were not paid, to burn the entire property, valued at $5,000,000. This was refused, as President Pierola issued a decree declaring it treason on the part of any one who furnished the enemy with money, punishable by confiscation. The Chilians burned this magnificent hacienda and destroyed all the machinery.

Whilst the Covadonga was blockading the small port of Chancay, north of Callao, on the 13th of September, an empty gig was seen adrift. A boat was sent to examine her. This was apparently thoroughly done; the gig was brought alongside, and tackles hooked to hoist her in. As soon as a strain was brought on the after-tackle a tremendous explosion took place; the Covadonga's side was blown in, causing her to sink almost immediately. It is supposed that this gig had been fitted with a false keel, packed with dynamite, and fitted with an igniter, which was connected with the after-tackle, so that no explosion could take place unless an effort was made actually to hoist in the boat.

September 16 two Chilian vessels visited the small port of Supe, about eighty miles north of Callao, capturing all the provisions in town, but doing no other damage.

Colonel Lynch's expeditionary force landed at Paita, the sea-port of Piura, the most northerly port of Peru, on the 18th of September, burning the custom-house and other valuable Government property.

September 22 the Cochrane and Tolten bombarded the town of Chorillos, a watering-place situated on the bay of the same name, and distant about nine miles southwest from Lima.

On the 23d of September the Chilians bombarded Chancay and the watering-place of Ancon, situated north of Callao.

October 26 the Huascar, which had been sent to Valparaiso to receive two new 180-pounder 8-inch breech-loading Armstrong guns of the latest type, arrived at Arica, and proceeded to rejoin the blockading squadron off Callao. Preparations were being made at Arica to transport the Chilian army north. Most of the troops were moved down from Tacna.

About November 1, Colonel Lynch's expeditionary force was landed at Quilca, with the intention of capturing Arequipa, but hearing that General Benegolea was still in that neighborhood with a strong force, a re-embarkation took place.

On the 3d of November the Huascar tried her new guns on the shore batteries at four-miles range. The Peruvians produced a new gun with a better range than any they had previously used.

November 9 all but two of the vessels blockading Callao went south to convoy the army transports north. Two transports landed about 2,000 Chilians on San Lorenzo Island, off Callao.

On the 18th of November about 7,000 Chilians were landed at Pisco, and marched to Chinchas. Pierola resigned the government to Señor la Puerta, and took command of the army in the field. The neutral fleet made preparations to shift its anchorage farther north, as it furnished a screen for the Chilian torpedo-boats at night and reconnaissances by day. Large numbers of refugees left for the north.

The blockading squadron off Callao on the 24th of November consisted of the Cochrane, Huascar, and Princess Louise.

A meeting of the foreign senior naval officers off Callao took place on the 25th of November. It was decided to take preliminary steps towards moving the refugee-hulks to Ancon, and to ask to be allowed to send representatives to the headquarters of both belligerents to note the progress of the war.

Lieutenant-Commander D. W. Mullan, of the Adams, was selected to accompany the Chilian headquarters, and went to Pisco in Her Britannic Majesty's ship Osprey, with representatives from the other senior officers. Lieutenant N. T. Houston, of the Lackawanna, was detailed to accompany General Pierola.

Early on the morning of December 6 three Chilian torpedo-launches were fired upon by a Peruvian armed tug. The Chilians immediately gave chase, and opened a hot fire from their machine-guns. The tug headed for the shore, returning the fire. As soon as the launches were in range the shore batteries opened on them, some of the shot falling very close to the neutral vessels. The Huascar and Princess Louise engaged the batteries to cover the launches. No damage was done on either side by the firing, except to the torpedo-launch Fresia, which was so badly damaged about the stern that she sank in fifteen fathoms of water, alongside of a vessel, off San Lorenzo, to which she had been secured by chains. Two additional torpedo-boats joined in the fight, but no attempt was made to use torpedoes.

On the 11th of December the monitor Atahualpa, accompanied by a tug, moved about a mile out from the mole. She was engaged by the Huascar, the Pilcomayo, Angamos, and Chacabuco, at long range. During the firing the 180-pounder breech-loading Armstrong (new model) of the Angamos flew bodily to the rear, slipping out of its trunnion-band and went overboard, killing a lieutenant belonging to one of the other ships (who had come aboard to take a few shots with the pet weapon), and the captain of the gun; wounding several of the men. A slight movement had been noticed between the gun and trunnion-band before this fire, but it was not considered to be of enough importance to warrant condemnation. This engagement had no important results.

By permission of the Chilian admiral the hulks were moved to Ancon, and were soon filled with refugees, as was the town.

The Chilian army for operations around Lima was commanded by General Baquedano, accompanied by His Excellency Don José Francisco Vergara, minister of war. It was organized in three divisions and a brigade of reserves. Each division consisted of two brigades. The artillery and cavalry were about equally divided between the divisions, none being held in reserve.

The First Division, numbering 8,241 men of all arms, was commanded by Captain Patricio Lynch, Chilian navy.

The Second Division, numbering 6,405 men of all arms, was commanded by General Sotomayor.

The Third Division, numbering 5,873 men of all arms, was commanded by Colonel D. Pedro Lagos.

The infantry numbered 21,008. The artillery 1,370, with twelve 12-pounder 7.5-centimeter breech-loading rifled Krupp campaign guns; six 9-pounder 2.5-inch breech-loading rifled Armstrongs; twenty-three 6-pounder 7.5-centimeter breech-loading rifled Krupp mountain guns; twelve 6-pounder 6-centimeter breech-loading rifled Krupp mountain guns; four 6-pounder 4-centimeter breech-loading rifled Krupp mountain guns, and six Gatling machine-guns, and about 1,200 horses. The cavalry, 1,251 men and horses.

The Reserve Brigade, numbering 3,110, consisting of the Second Regulars, Valparaiso (gendarmerie), Zapadores (engineers), and Quilotta Battalion, giving a grand total of 23,621 men and 63 guns.

A mining or torpedo party accompanied the army, whose duty it was to search for and remove mines, or, if forced to act on the defensive, to place them.

On the 18th of November, as we have before stated, the First Division of the Chilian army, then under command of General Villegran, landed at Pisco, the First Brigade, under Captain Lynch, remaining in the small town at the port, the general taking up his quarters with the Second Brigade in Pisco proper, situated about 3 miles inland. The Fourth Regulars and a battery of artillery, under Colonel Amunatigui, commanding the Second Brigade, moved to Ica, situated about 45 miles inland, and connected with Pisco by rail. On the 1st of December the First Brigade of the Second Division, under Colonel Gana, arrived at Pisco. On the afternoon of the 13th of December, the First Division having been assembled at Pisco, started to march north by a road running along the sea-shore. They reached Tambo-de Mora at 9 a. m. the next morning, a distance of only 18 miles, having made but five short halts. After a halt until the 18th, Lynch's brigade again started up the coast. General Villegran with the Second Brigade was ordered to return to Pisco, General Baquedano being probably displeased with the slow advance up the coast. Villegran was relieved of his command, which was given to Captain Lynch. On the 20th of December the Second and Third Divisions, and on the 24th the Second Brigade of the First Division, left Pisco, and landed at Chilca and Curayaco, afterward occupying the towns of Lurin and Pachacamac. The landing was very expeditiously carried out, the regular ship's boats being assisted by the large flats which most of the ships carried, these being capable of carrying one hundred men at a time with all their belongings. The road from Chilca to Lurin, about 15 miles distant, was very sandy, and all transportation had to be done by packing. The army went into camp about Lurin, where the headquarters were established, except the Second Brigade of the Second Division, which was posted at Pachacamac, distant about 3 miles from Lurin, and covering its approach from the mountains. Gana's brigade of the First Division was thrown across the river Lurin to protect the approaches from Chorillos, and to cover a bridge which had been left standing, and by which the army would have to cross. Comfortable shelter-huts were constructed by the troops out of palm leaves and sugar-cane. These were needed only for protection against the sun and dew, as it never rains in this part of the world. The time was devoted to drilling and to target practice for both infantry and artillery. On the 27th of December a portion of Barboza's brigade encountered Colonel Sevilla's Rimac regiment of Peruvian cavalry, which had been giving Captain Lynch's brigade much trouble on his march north. Sevilla, thinking Pachacamac unoccupied, intended to go to Lima by the pass of the same name. The action was quite severe. Sevilla was killed, and two hundred of his men either killed or captured; the remainder succeeded in cutting their way through, and reached Lima in safety.

On the 6th of January General Baquedano, with five hundred cavalry, five hundred mounted infantry, and a platoon of artillery, reconnoitered the Peruvian lines before Chorillos, about 7 miles distant from Lurin. Some artillery firing took place. The whole Peruvian line was thoroughly felt and located.

On Sunday, January 9, Colonel Barboza, with several hundred men from his brigade, reconnoitered the town of Até, approaching to within 4 miles of Lima. A slight skirmish took place.

At 5.30 p. m., January 12, the whole army was put in motion to take up its position during the night before the Peruvian lines. All but the Coquimbo and Mezpilla regiments, which were to act as a reserve for the left wing, moved by what is known as the Atocongo road—an almost impassable trail through the passes of the mountains—considered impracticable by the Peruvian commanders. This pass approached at right angles to the Peruvian left. At 2.30 on the morning of January 13 the Chilian army was massed in the end of the pass ready to fall upon the Peruvians, who were utterly ignorant of their danger. Most of the Chilian field artillery, with the reserve infantry of the left wing, had approached by the shore to within fighting distance of the Peruvian center. The mountain batteries accompanied their respective brigades.

Let us now see how the Peruvians were prepared to meet the storm that was about to break upon them.

The landing of the Chilians at Chilca, on the 22d of December, found the Peruvians, although certainly forewarned, not forearmed. The army of Lima was an army only in name. There was no organized commissariat, the men were poorly clothed and worse shod, many of the regiments being left to shoe themselves with sandals made of the undressed skins of the cattle given them to eat. The small-arms procured from the United States, Remington's, Peabody-Martini's, Evans's, and Winchester's, were in most cases so rusted and glued with bad oil that they had become almost useless. The cavalry were a little better than the infantry, but the horses were poor. The artillery, armed with all manner of guns, some of them obsolete in pattern, others made on untried principles, by private firms in Lima, and totally without practice in the field, were poorly fitted to compete with the veteran, well-armed artillery of the Chilians.

The Reserves, some 7,000 in number, could hardly be called soldiers, but on account of their superior intelligence and the fact that they were fighting for their homes, they should have been more trustworthy than the volunteers. They were the men of Lima called out by a degree. They were supposed to have been drilled every day, and were ordered to sleep in their barracks at night.

The Regular Army, numbering 26,500 men of all arms, was divided into four divisions of about 6,000 men each, commanded by Colonels Iglesias, Suarez, Davila, and Caceris; the Reserves by Colonel Echiniqui. The whole number of the Army of Lima was about 33,500 men.

Up to this time but little had been done for the protection of the rich city of Lima. Redoubts, mounted with a few heavy guns, had been erected on the summit of Mount St. Christobal to the north, and Mount San Bartolomé to the south. One or two batteries had been thrown up on the small hills south of the city. Two redoubts had been commenced near the town of Miraflores.

December 23, the First and Second Divisions, under Colonels Iglesias and Suarez, moved to Chorillos, and the next day the Third, Fourth, and Reserves, under Colonels Davila, Caceris, and Echiniqui, the first two going to the Chorillos line, the latter to Miraflores, about 3 miles nearer Lima, Chorillos being about 8 miles from that city.

The plan of the Peruvian commanders was to act on the defensive, as they had done throughout the war. For defensive purposes the line selected was magnificent. Chorillos, which is quite a large town, containing many fine summer residences, is situated at the southern end of the bay of the same name, on the edge of the plain of Lima, which descends precipitously to the sea. Immediately to the southward of the town is a range of hills called the Salto del Fraile. The western side of this range juts out into the sea and forms Point Solar, the southern boundary of Chorillos Bay; the eastern side slopes down into a valley that connects the plain of Lima with a sandy desert; the southern side connects the Salto with this desert. The valley referred to is about three miles wide. In it is the town of Villa. The eastern side of this valley is formed by the end of a range of high hills that extend in a north-northeast direction for about 4 miles, where a break occurs, forming a second valley, which leads towards San Juan; then the hills recommence, and extend about 3 miles in a northeast direction to Monterico Chico, where they meet and are flanked by the coast range, in a spur of which we left the Chilian army massed for the attack. The slope of this crescent of hills towards the Chilians was steep and very sandy; the reverse slope was gradual and firm. The Peruvian Regulars were formed in one line on the crest of these hills, extending from Villa to Monterico Chico, a distance of 8 miles. Strong trenches three feet deep, four feet wide, and with a sand-bag parapet two feet high, were dug along the whole crest. The valley of San Juan, about a quarter of a mile wide, was protected by field batteries and Gatlings placed behind earthworks on small hills, retired a little from the general line. The left flank was supposed to be thoroughly protected by the coast range, and the right flank, where the main attack was expected and where the best troops were posted, was covered by heavy batteries on the Salto del Fraile. Distributed along the whole line of intrenchments, in commanding positions, were between 60 and 70 guns and mitrailleuses. The four divisions of Peruvian Regulars were posted in regular order from right to left, part of the First Division manning the heights of the Salto del Fraile. The advanced slope along the whole line was thickly planted with torpedoes. About 4½ miles in rear of this first line, and almost parallel to it, was a second line, manned by Colonel Echiniqui's 7,000 Reserves. This line, which extended across the plain of Lima from the sea to the mountains, consisted of five redoubts connected by earthworks and adobe fences prepared for defense. All the fences in front of the line to a distance of about 500 yards were leveled, but beyond that they were left standing, to prove in the end perfect breastworks for the Chilians. In the redoubts of this line a number of heavy guns were mounted, and, as an additional protection to the right flank, which was cut by the railroad from Chorillos to Lima, a platform-car had been converted into a movable battery, mounted with light guns and propelled by a locomotive. The town of Miraflores was situated in rear of the right of this line.

As has been the remarkable custom in this war, the Peruvians had almost no outposts. It is true a company or so was thrown a few hundred yards to the front, and from it a small picket was posted a little more to the front.

General Pierola established his headquarters in Chorillos, and is said to have been indefatigable in his efforts to prepare his army for the coming contest. He seems not to have been wanting in zeal or in personal courage. The ignorance of the Peruvians in regard to the force, position, and movements of their enemy seems almost marvelous. With the exception of one reconnaissance down the Atocongo Pass, in which he satisfied himself that the very road by which the Chilians advanced was impassable, he never moved beyond his lines.

On the 2d of January 1,500 of the police force of Lima, who, on account of their services in several revolutions, were considered almost the flower of the army, were brought to the front, and posted at San Juan, and 500 more were sent up the Oroya road to Matucana, to prevent an advance of the Chilians from that direction. In order to replace the police, the Urban Guard, consisting of about 2,500 foreigners of all nationalities, and commanded by a retired captain in the French navy, was called out. The Government, however, recalled 300 of the police, and disbanded the guard on the 9th.

On the 3d of January an unsuccessful attempt was made to blow up the Huascar; a tug was fitted with a Lay torpedo for the purpose. Instead of attacking the Huascar, the officer in charge took the tug into Ancon Bay, where he destroyed the torpedo and beached his vessel. Here she was discovered, and entirely demolished the next morning by the Pilcomayo, Tolten, and a torpedo-boat. The Chilian shells set fire to a portion of the town of Ancon. Some Peruvian Reserves, and the guns of the railroad battery previously referred to, which had been run down the Ancon road, replied to the fire, but without effect.

On the 9th, Colonel Barboza's reconnaissance to Até was reported to Pierola as a movement of 4,000 men to turn his flank by the Manchay Pass. This caused an increase of the troops on the left of the line, and the posting of a battery of light artillery on a hill a little in advance of the left flank, where it commanded the entrance to the pass.

On the 10th the day of battle was considered to be near by the Peruvian commanders, as small pickets of Chilians were reported in sight on the plain and surrounding hills. Still no additional precautions were taken to guard against surprise.

We left the Chilian army massed in the pass of Manchay at 2.30 a. m., January 13. At about this time General Baquedano and his staff arrived, and took up their position on a commanding eminence. The First Division was to attack the Peruvian right, the Second the center at San Juan, and the Third the left, from San Juan to Monterico Chico. The Reserve Brigade, under Lieutenant-Colonel Aristides Martinez was to cover with the artillery the attack of the Second and Third Divisions. At dawn, about 5 a. m., Lynch's division gained a position 400 yards in front of the Peruvian right before it was discovered, and at first a straggling fire opened on it, which changed to a heavy fire, from both sides, along the whole line as the Second and Third Chilian Divisions came into position. The fighting became general. A few torpedoes exploded, wounding many of the men and exasperating the survivors to fury. The Second Division, covered by the Reserves, carried the town of San Juan at about 6 o'clock, many of the Peruvians, notably the Lima police, throwing down their arms and flying at the first charge. The artillery was very little used on either side, except that on the Salto del Fraile, which played on the Chilian left with great effect. The center having been cut, the Peruvian left was driven from its position and towards Miraflores. Shortly afterwards the right, being flanked by the Chilian center, and attacked in front by the whole First Division, was driven back to the Salto del Fraile and Chorillos. The Chilian cavalry, charging through the San Juan Valley, accelerated the flight of the Peruvian center and left. A large number of men belonging to the corps forming this portion of the line arrived in Lima that afternoon without arms.

The First Peruvian Division, under Colonel Iglesias, the secretary of war, now occupied the houses and garden-walls of Chorillos. There they were attacked by the First Chilian Division, which was repulsed with great loss. The Chilians were now strongly re-enforced by troops from the other divisions and by most of the artillery. Not a man came to the rescue of the Peruvians, who, at the next assault, were driven back with great loss in killed, wounded, and prisoners, among the latter their brave commander, to the batteries on the hills. These were soon assaulted on all sides, and at 2 p. m. the Chilians were in possession of the field of battle, with the whole Peruvian First Division and many more as prisoners.

The Peruvian loss in this day's fighting amounted to 1,500 killed; wounded, 2,500; prisoners, 4,000; 5 standards and 70 pieces of artillery. The total Chilian loss amounted to about 3,000 men.

The Chilians now rested on their laurels. The whole Chilian army was massed in and about Chorillos, instead of immediately taking up a position in opposition to the still complete second line of the Peruvians. Considerable demoralization, probably attributable to the large amount of liquor in the shops, ensued. Had General Pierola taken advantage of this condition of affairs with the large army still under his command, most of which was entirely fresh, and perhaps eager to revenge its disgrace and defend its homes, Lima might have been rescued.

During the forenoon of January 14 General Baquedano sent Don Isidoro Errazuris, secretary to the Chilian minister of war, and Colonel Iglesias, the captured Peruvian minister of war, through the Peruvian lines by flag of truce to General Pierola with a proposition that, if the Peruvian army were disbanded, he would treat for peace on the basis of the Arica conference, with certain additions warranted by the present position of his forces. It was further stated that if this proposition was not acceded to hostilities would recommence, and Lima, if captured, would be sacked and burned. The envoys returned, and later in the afternoon another Chilian officer was sent to receive the answer, which was that the proposition could not be entertained.

Later in the day General Pierola sent to Lima requesting a conference with the foreign diplomatic corps, a committee of which body soon responded to the invitation. After conferring with General Pierola, two foreign officers, under a flag of truce, were sent to General Baquedano to request an interview, which was arranged for 7 a. m. January 15.

An armistice was agreed to, to extend until midnight. The committee then returned to Miraflores, and thence went to Lima, returning to Miraflores with the whole diplomatic corps and the senior foreign naval officers at a few minutes after 2 p. m.

During the forenoon the Chilian army had been moved, and two battalions of the Third Division, with some of the light artillery, had been placed quite near to the Peruvian right. The Peruvian line consisted of about 5,000 Reserves, with 15,000 Regulars from the first line, some of whom had been captured in Lima and sent back to the front. On the extreme right was a Naval Brigade, organized from the crews of the men-of-war at Callao.

At about 2.30 p. m., whilst General Pierola was at lunch with the foreign naval officers, and the diplomats were waiting for the conference, General Baquedano rode up to the front of the Chilian line and ordered the whole of his Third Division to deploy into line parallel to the Peruvian right and extend to the sea-shore. The Chilian ships, which had taken no part in the first day's fight, were anchored a little to the northward of Miraflores, their guns enfilading the Peruvian position. Whilst superintending the deployment, General Baquedano approached quite close to that part of the line where the Peruvian men-of-war's men were posted. A few shots were fired—it is asserted—by them, they not understanding the condition of affairs; this was followed by a gun from one of the redoubts, and soon a general fire was opened along the whole line. This was an entire surprise to the commanders on both sides. The Chilians, who were engaged in preparing their dinners—many being dispersed in search of water and wood—were taken entirely by surprise, and a panic ensued, which was only checked by the timely arrival of the Reserve Brigade. The Chilian fleet now opened fire, but directed most of its attention to the town of Miraflores. The Peruvian Reserves fought well, and succeeded in repelling an assault on the right redoubt at about 3.30 p. m. The First Division now re-enforced the Third, whilst the Second Brigade of the Second Division maneuvered to turn the Peruvian right flank. Thus re-enforced, an assault was made on the right redoubt, which was carried, and the Peruvian right doubled back on the center. In the mean while a Chilian light battery gained an eminence to the left of the Peruvian left, and opened a galling enfilading fire on the line. The Chilian First Division, covered by a strong force of artillery and cavalry, continued to push towards the Peruvian left, carrying one after another the remaining four redoubts, two of which were blown up by mines, without, however, doing great damage. Some of the Peruvian battalions fought well, but many, with their officers, retreated, throwing away their arms without firing a shot. The Chilian Carabineros cavalry regiment charged repeatedly with Señor Vergara, the minister of war, at its head. By 5 p. m. the whole Peruvian army was fleeing towards Lima, badly beaten and entirely demoralized. From this moment the Peruvian army disappeared, some going to the mountains to their homes, others to Ancon; those who remained in Lima exchanged their uniforms for less conspicuous clothing and mingled with the people. The loss of the Chilians amounted in all to two thousand men, that of the Peruvians must have been still greater, but will probably never be accurately ascertained. All the arms, ammunition, guns, &c., belonging to the Peruvian army fell into the hands of the Chilians. The town of Miraflores was entirely burned. General Pierola, with a few friends, retired to the town of Chocas, situated about 35 miles from Lima.

The Chilians did not move on the city of Lima after the battle, probably, on account of the fear of the commander-in-chief that the scenes of Chorillos would be repeated in Lima.

The inhabitants of Lima were in a terrible state of excitement, fearing the Chilians, fearing the violence of their own mob, which had been largely recruited by the stragglers from the army, and not reassured by the fact that General Lacotera, minister of war under Prado, had, at this dark hour, attempted by a revolution to seize the supreme power. Lacotera was not successful, and was placed a prisoner on board of the Union, from which vessel he escaped.

The legations were full of women and children, fifteen hundred having collected in the house of our minister. Ancon was so full of refugees that, after filling the hulks and foreign men-of-war, it was found necessary to break open the houses of the town. Bedding, old sails, and provisions were issued from the ships, and a strong guard of foreign men-of-war's men was maintained in the town. By the latter all armed refugees were disarmed; these were well generally provided with ammunition, but in many cases it was found that men carrying Remington caliber .50 rifles were supplied with Peabody-Martini .45 caliber cartridges, and *vice versa*, and it was learned that this condition of affairs had existed on the battle-field.

There was no serious disturbance in Lima Sunday morning, January 16, but in the afternoon small knots of armed men, composed principally of deserters and negroes, were seen in the streets. Occasional discharges of fire-arms were heard, which increased during the evening to a regular fusilade. At 9 p. m. an attack was made on the Chinese quarter, which was soon looted and in flames. The mob then began to loot and burn the liquor stores and small shops, many of which belonged to foreigners, principally to Italians. During the night fires were to be seen all over the city. Several attempts on the part of the foreign fire brigade to take out their engines were frustrated by attacks of the mob. As there was no government and no police, the mob had nothing to oppose it.

Whilst these scenes were enacting in Lima, still more serious ones were transpiring in Callao. There the mob burned or blew up the ships and batteries, destroying, as far as they were able, the guns and all public property. It then turned its attention to the town, as in Lima. Late in the night the foreigners managed to get together, and taking advantage of the drunken condition of many of the disturbers, they succeeded in making a stand against them, and finally restored order, not, however, without wreaking terrible vengeance on their despoilers.

In Lima, on Monday morning, the Urban Guard succeeded in reorganizing, and by going energetically to work finally succeeded in clearing the streets of the mob whilst the fire companies put out the fires. A detachment of the Urban Guard was sent to take possession of Fort San Cristobal.

The diplomatic corps and senior naval commanders had met on Sunday morning and had arranged a capitulation of the city, by the terms of which the Chilians were to take possession on Monday at noon with a sufficient force only to insure tranquility and safety to the inhabitants.

At 4.30 p. m. on Monday, the 17th day of January, the Urban Guard received the column of occupation, and the city was formally surrendered to General Saavedra, inspector-general of the Chilian army, who had been detailed as military governor of Lima. The forces detailed to guard the city were the First Regulars, Bulnes Battalion (Santiago policemen), the Cazadores and Caribineros de Yungai cavalry regiments, and three batteries of light artillery. These relieved the foreign police.

On Tuesday Captain Lynch, with his division, occupied Callao, of which place he had been appointed military governor.

The remainder of the Chilian army was encamped in the fields and quartered in the haciendas about Lima, with the exception of two battalions which were sent up the Oroya road.

On Thursday, at 3.30 p. m., the Chilian flag was hoisted, with some ceremony, on the palace, which was now the headquarters of the army of occupation.

Shortly after the surrender of Lima General Baquedano, with all but about 10,000 of his troops, returned to Chili. Admiral Riveros, with most of the ships, also withdrew, leaving Captain La Torre in command on the Peruvian coast.

Since the fall of Lima there has been no battle of importance; many skirmishes have taken place between portions of the army of occupation and small bodies of Peruvians. There has also been a large amount of diplomatic maneuvering, which, although belonging to history, conveys no lesson of value to the naval or military student.

THEO. B. M. MASON,
Lieutenant U. S. Navy.

www.ingramcontent.com/pod-product-compliance
Lightning Source LLC
Chambersburg PA
CBHW020226090426
42735CB00010B/1604